CW01510709

Confronting Postmaternal Thinki

Theresa Miller

Julie Stephens

CONFRONTING POSTMATERNAL THINKING

Feminism, Memory, and Care

———————————

Columbia University Press   New York

Columbia University Press

Publishers Since 1893

New York Chichester, West Sussex

Copyright © 2011 Columbia University Press

All rights reserved

Library of Congress Cataloging-in-Publication Data

Stephens, Julie, 1956–

Confronting postmaternal thinking : feminism, memory, and care / Julie
Stephens.

p. cm.

Includes bibliographical references and index.

ISBN 978-0-231-14920-4 (cloth: alk. paper) —ISBN 978-0-231-14921-1 (pbk.:
alk. paper) —ISBN 978-0-231-52056-0 (e-book)

1. Feminist theory. 2. Motherhood—Social aspects. 3. Motherhood—
Political aspects. 4. Collective memory. I. Title.

HQ1190.S754   2011

306.874'301—dc23   2011025624

Casebound editions of Columbia University Press books are printed on
permanent and durable acid-free paper.

Printed in the United States of America

c 10 9 8 7 6 5 4 3 2 1

p 10 9 8 7 6 5 4 3 2 1

References to Internet Web sites (URLs) were accurate at the time of writing. Neither the author nor Columbia University Press is responsible for
Web sites that may have expired or changed since the book was prepared.

In memory of Eliza Jean Odgers 1896–1993

Contents

Preface

We pick the questions we study, all of us at least
in part, to preserve or enhance things we revere or love.

ARLIE RUSSELL HOCHSCHILD, "Feeling Capitalism"

This book is an attempt to bring the maternal into scholarly focus in an unconventional way. It aims to confront an increasingly widespread cultural unease, if not hostility, toward certain expressions of the maternal and maternalist political perspectives in general. Broadly defined, maternalism is the application of values, usually associated with mothering, to the society as a whole. According to this view, the principles of nurture, care, and protection are suffused with rich ethical and political meanings and offer an alternative conception of the social. However, maternalist ideas have long been in decline and often provoke unease and antagonism, especially when raised in a feminist context.[1] I will argue that this unease is linked to a much deeper cultural anxiety around nurture, care, and dependency. While motherhood has always borne the weight of cultural ambivalence and tension, there appears to be a new way of thinking about mothers and mothering that amplifies this anxiety and gives it a different shape. I call this contemporary reconfiguration *postmaternal thinking*. What follows is an effort to identify and critically reflect on some of the consequences of this pervasive cultural development.

Postmaternal thinking refers to a process where the ideals intimately bound up with the practices of mothering are disavowed in the public sphere, and conflicted in the private. In my view this is a profoundly regressive development with significant political and social effects. What unfolds then is the proposition that postmaternal thinking is a prevailing cultural logic, central not only to policy debates but also to contemporary understandings of feminism and to the role that care, nurture, and dependency inevitably plays in all our lives.

Unlike studies that lay the blame for negative conceptions of mothering at the feet of second-wave feminists, my analysis gives a central role to neoliberalism, a system of ideas, concrete policies, and modes of governance that have shaped the world's economic and political agenda for almost a quarter of a century. Given the antagonism expressed by many conservatives in the United States toward what is perceived to be liberalism, some conflate the term *neoliberalism* with a variety of left liberalisms. In order to avoid any such confusion, it is crucial to stress that neoliberalism has a quite different meaning and association and is widely used in public discourse, especially outside the American context. The term usually refers to the way liberal doctrines of individual responsibility, small government, and a self-regulating market resurfaced in the 1980s and were given a new global inflection and reach. The idea of neoliberalism also signals transformations in the labor market such as the increasing casualization of labor, economic deregulation, the global mobility of capital, the privatization of state services, and changing patterns of paid and unpaid work by women. Sometimes these changes are referred to as "the new capitalism" or "the new economy." However, these expressions can risk concealing key philosophical and social shifts by their emphasis on the economic and political. The term *neoliberalism*, by contrast, seems to include all of these elements.

It is important to point out that my interest lies in the ideological dimensions of neoliberalism: the changed understandings of self, gender, citizenship, and the state that have accompanied and sustained different processes of neoliberal restructuring. While a more detailed

as (19th idealized the autonomous. indiv & the idea of Self-Help

examination of these changes and their role in postmaternal thinking will be proposed in chapter 1, a good starting point for a definition of the aspect of neoliberalism to be discussed here is a system of belief that idealizes the "entrepreneurial citizen engaged in paid employment."[2] Consequently, a significant theme of this book will be how the valorization of individual self-sufficiency has become a dominant cultural logic or ethos with ramifications for mothers, and others, who are giving and receiving care.

Any current discussion of neoliberalism inevitably raises the specter of the global financial crisis of 2008–2010. There have been many premature pronouncements about the death of neoliberalism in the wake of the collapse of large financial institutions and the subsequent "bail out" of banks and corporations by national governments.[3] As the examples discussed in this book will attest, neoliberal ideals still saturate the public discourse, particularly where gendered issues of care, nurture, and dependency are concerned. In fact, in the words of Shelley Gavigan and Dorothy Chunn, the current crisis provides "a window of opportunity for critical scholars and activists to attempt to reframe debates about social welfare, work and equality and to reassert the discourse of social justice into the public consciousness and political agendae of liberal democracies."[4] I hope this book can be viewed as one response to this opportunity.

To delineate and understand contemporary repudiations of the maternal, I have taken a deliberately interdisciplinary approach. I therefore draw on a diverse range of literary, sociological, feminist, and philosophical sources. However, my approach differs from other studies of feminism or neoliberalism (or the intersection of the two) by critically applying new insights from the area of "memory studies" to this contested field. By looking at maternalism through the lens of cultural memory theory, a very different picture emerges to that of previous scholarly work, including the more recent literature on the topic of how feminism has been remembered.

I will argue that postmaternal thinking relies on an elaborate process of cultural forgetting. This process includes the forgetting of ideals

see Robert McRuer on devalued domesticity.

which results in the 'forgetting' of certain texts that present alternative maternalism linked to maternal forms of care and the figure of the nurturing mother. However, this is not primarily a book about motherhood. There is a rich and burgeoning scholarship in this area, and, although I engage with these sources at various points, my purpose here is a different one. I am aware of the risks of investigating shared cultural assumptions rather than documenting the concrete experiences of specific mothers or the contexts that shape the particular ways they may relate to their children's needs. I hope any concerns about this approach will be addressed in the chapters to follow.

Throughout the writing process, I have returned to Sara Ruddick's definitive study *Maternal Thinking: Toward A Politics of Peace.*[5] The concept of postmaternal thinking is a deliberate reference, and a tribute to Ruddick's work. Her deeply philosophical reasoning about the special cognitive capacities, metaphysical attitudes, and ethical conceptions that arise from mothering continues to have a wide impact. Reading and rereading Sara Ruddick twenty-one years after the publication of her influential book, I was repeatedly struck by the marked originality of her ideas and their significant contemporary resonance. When faced with any impasse in the course of my own writing, turning back to *Maternal Thinking* always provided a way through to new and fresh insights.

Sara Ruddick took a warm intellectual interest in my book. Her correspondence during the course of its writing was generous, engaged, and penetrating. Her untimely death in March 2011 marks a significant loss to feminist philosophy and to all scholars grappling with questions of care, feminist ethics, nonviolence, and peace. At a personal level, I am immensely saddened by her death. I will always be grateful for the support she gave me in what turned out to be the last year of her life. I had looked forward to meeting her and thanking her in person. Given that this is no longer possible, I sincerely hope that my contribution to thinking about the maternal will widen recognition of Ruddick's work and legacy.

I have been asked whether personal narratives about my own experiences as a mother would be included in this analysis of postmaternal thinking and contemporary maternalism. While I have enormous admiration for those authors who successfully combine the social, political, theoretical, and the personal,[6] I do not attempt such a task here. Certain conceptual and methodological frameworks lend themselves more to this approach than others. I rely instead on a range of different narratives of maternal experience. This includes feminist memoir, confessional life writing, blogs, biography, media commentary, and oral testimony. Despite the fact that my personal experience does not explicitly feature as having representational status in this book, it lurks in the book's shadows, and the subject position in my writing is that of someone caught in the same tensions and contradictions that are identified between care and paid work, autonomy and connectedness, difference or equality, memory and forgetting. Productively exploring these tensions has shaped the call for an alternative feminist maternalism in my conclusion.

It is crucial to emphasize the link between feminism and maternalism in the discussion of political alternatives that is to emerge in these pages. My book is not situated within an antifeminist popular revival of domesticity or renewed discourses about the moral mother. Naomi Mezey and Cornelia T. Pillard mount a persuasive critique of this current trend in the U.S., citing the way Sarah Palin plays the "mother card" in her political interventions. They refer to Palin's invocation of mother grizzly bears rising up to protect their young as a way of mobilizing conservative women. Interestingly, Palin's "Mama Grizzlies" are depicted alongside Web-based organizations such as Moms Rising, all examples of a new and regressive maternalism. The authors argue that this new maternalism reinforces traditional familial gender roles and undermines both the legal equality of women and the domestic equality of men.[7] The contrast between this version of maternal politics and Ruddick's conception of maternal thinking could not be starker. While I completely disagree with many of the premises in "Against the New Maternalism," the provocative analysis of Mezey and Pillard deserves considered attention and is addressed in subsequent chapters. In keeping with my commitment to feminist care ethics, it should be noted that the completion of this book has been both constrained and enriched by caring for family members facing serious illness and incapacity. This has brought questions of human vulnerability into sharp focus and fostered a renewed commitment to an interconnected, relational sense of self, albeit remembering that, in a cultural context where care is both devalued and gendered, this can never be without tension and ambivalence. It has also strengthened my belief that the issue of providing women and men with better opportunities to arrange their lives around care will not be resolved ethically by simply outsourcing everyday care and emotional labor to a private market or through piecemeal policy initiatives.

My thanks for support at various stages of the writing process go to a number of people. At Columbia University Press, my particular thanks to Wendy Lochner, senior executive editor, who not only responded to my proposal within a day but also put considerable effort into convincing others that this would prove to be a worthy book. Also at Columbia University Press, Christine Mortlock and Susan Pensak have provided vital assistance throughout this long process. I would like to acknowledge the support of the National Library of Australia and Victoria University. The opportunity to take up a Harold White Fellowship introduced me to the exceptional Oral History and Manuscript Collections at the library and also to the expertise of key staff such as Margy Burn, Kevin Bradley, and Marie-Louise Ayres. Delving into feminist oral history also led me to iconic second-wave feminists Sara Dowse, Biff Ward, and Suzanne Bellamy, who all provided valuable input, enthusiasm, and support just when I needed it. Thanks also extend to Merrindahl Andrew, Marian Sawer, and Margaret Henderson. Renee Armstrong offered bibliographic assistance when it was most required. Arena has also been an important reference point, shaping my thinking in a number of key areas. I am also indebted to Daniel Davis for raising other kinds of memory questions with such sensitivity and insight. These questions assisted in less obvious but crucial ways during the final stages of writing.

For many years I have had generous encouragement from social philosopher and fellow child-centered feminist Anne Manne. She has been particularly supportive of this book. Her incisive intellectual insights, shared unease with market relations and her friendship have played a central role in developing my ideas. All of Anne Manne's writing has been a radical resistance to postmaternal thinking. If, as Arlie Hochschild suggests, we pick the things we study to preserve or enhance the things we love, then this book owes its existence to the people closest to me. Thanks go to my mother Margaret Stephens and my sister Lenore Stephens. My son Emile Frankel has taught me to "think maternally," and he expands my understanding of love and care on a daily basis. Finally, profound gratitude goes to my partner Boris Frankel who has provided constant intellectual engagement, critical reading, scholarly advice, compulsive honesty, humor, and loving care. As always, Boris has helped me keep the most important things firmly in perspective. The book is dedicated to the memory of my grandmother, Eliza Jean Odgers, and to her fierce and enabling maternal love.

Confronting Postmaternal Thinking

Introduction

Were the day to come when women's oppression was eradicated,
would we also wish to eradicate caring for others?

CAROL J. ADAMS, "Caring About Suffering"

istening to the radio during a blistering summer when the death toll from heat and bushfire was unprecedented, I was struck by an odd discussion of a book that promised to teach the skill and etiquette of how to be "kind and compassionate in a moment of illness."[1] The author, Susan Halpern, offered advice about how to be at ease with a loved one who is gravely ill and identified the emotional challenges posed by visiting a seriously sick friend. The expertise required to manage such a situation was presented as something we needed to relearn. Apparently we once knew how to respond with care and attentiveness to illness, but now we are in danger of making serious mistakes. Caring was invoked as a set of skills to be acquired and performed without the intrusion of unruly or extreme displays of emotion. The gendered dimensions of this issue, women being both the participants and the intended audience, were ignored. Nor did the radio discussion question why the capacity for care is perceived as having been so thoroughly forgotten. It did illustrate, however, a wider cultural anxiety around nurture, human dependency, caregiving, and emotion. This cultural anxiety is at the heart of what I am calling postmaternal thinking.

I begin with this case because it links a reported unease about care and nurture to the problem of memory. The apparent "not remembering" how to tend a loved one is addressed, in this instance via regulatory ideas about skills and retraining. Yet the underlying amnesia seems to be a much broader phenomenon concerning the fact that dependency is inescapable in the life history of each person, as feminist philosopher and ethicist Eva Feder Kittay so clearly reminds us.[2] What is revealed in these discourses on forgetting? Theorists of cultural memory throw some light on such questions by demonstrating that the content, sources, and experiences that are "recalled, forgotten, or suppressed" are "intricately bound up with issues of power and hegemony."[3] In the pages to follow, certain conceptions of cultural memory will be crucial as the lens through which postmaternal thinking is viewed. One of the central aims of this book will be to develop, and carefully build up, a picture of postmaternal thinking. The starting point for a definition will be an exploration of various ways the maternal and the values associated with maternal forms of care have been largely rejected in the public sphere and marginalized or conflicted in the private domain. I will argue that the privatization of maternal ideas, ethics, and forms of selfhood has had profound social and political consequences. Moreover, diminishing the public relevance of mothering as a model for social forms of care has also taken a toll on the personal lives of women. It has shaped contemporary ways feminism has been remembered and, unfortunately contributed to the current dominance of what I will suggest is a degendered form of feminism. In short, postmaternal thinking functions like a prevailing ideology. It is a cultural distortion that reinforces unjust social relations, hides the significance of gendered care, and inhibits different ways of imagining social and political alternatives.

It is important to distinguish my approach to the postmaternal from the pioneering work that is being done on postmaternalism by feminist social theorist Ann Orloff in the social policy arena.[4] Orloff's impressive contribution to our understanding of issues of gender in the welfare restructuring of the 1990s cannot be overstated. While the term *postmaternalism* is not in wide currency, Orloff deftly employs the term to describe the policy moves away from the political support for women's caregiving roles as mothers to gender-neutral notions of recognizing support only for economically "active" adults.[5] The programs around "welfare-to-work" common in most advanced democracies today are but one example of this policy shift. According to Orloff, there has been a "farewell to maternalism" in formerly "gendered" policy regimes. This is a process where women's claims as *mothers* have lost their political authority. Legitimacy is only conferred on women's claims *workers* or *citizens*.[6] These ideas will be discussed in more detail in the following chapter. Suffice it to say here, my use of the concept of postmaternal thinking not only draws on Orloff's scholarship but also elaborates and extends it beyond a social policy perspective.

Policy-centric or state-centric approaches, particularly in studies of the maternalist campaigns of the late nineteenth and early part of the twentieth century, are fundamental to our understanding of the history of the welfare state and the recent restructuring of social provision for women and children. *Maternalism* is a highly disputed term in this growing literature.[7] To some it is defined as an orientation among early women reformers which involved the belief that their experience as mothers gave them moral authority and expertise in the area of providing for the poor. According to this perspective, maternalists also positioned themselves as mothers of future generations and therefore as those most qualified to speak about future social policy. Other scholars advance a different view of maternalist campaigns and the crucial role they played in state formation across America. Some definitions are rather broad and refer to policies by women, for women,[8] while others denote a quite specific ideology revolving around the ideas of mothers benefiting the state by raising its citizen/workers and the notion that women, at the global level, are "united across class, race, and nation by their common capacity for motherhood and therefore share a responsibility for the world's children."[9] Conflicts arise in this literature about whether maternalism was class-based and racialized or more universal in its reach. Related disputes also include arguments about the traditional, male breadwinner model of the family (promoted by "conservative" maternalists) or interpretations that highlight the more progressive elements in maternalist ideas. What is common to these views is the recognition of the significant role that beliefs about gender difference played in the politics of maternalism and a shared sense of how contested and ambiguous early maternalist politics tended to be.

Any definition of maternalism, whether of the historical or contemporary variety, is premised on an assertion of the public, social importance of motherhood and the nurture and care of children. For the purposes of this study, I will be reworking definitions advanced by Seth Koven and Sonya Michel, two key historians of women's welfare activism, in their celebrated comparative collection *Mothers of a New World: Maternalist Politics and the Origins of Welfare States.*[10] The authors develop a persuasive and influential conception of maternalism as a discourse, an ideology, and a set of practices that transformed motherhood from women's primary *private* responsibility to *public* policy (2). In their own words, "we apply the term to ideologies and discourses that exalted women's capacity to mother and applied to society as a whole, the values they attached to that role: care, nurturance and morality" (4). As will become evident, the insights provided by Koven and Michel have strong relevance to the concept of postmaternal thinking and the discussion of the possibilities of a new maternalism to follow. This is because the authors acknowledge that maternalist perspectives can go beyond the policy arena and generate "searching critiques of state and society" (2). Such a politics, at its best, can challenge the boundaries between public and private, men and women, state and civil society (6). Koven is also at pains to demonstrate that maternalist discourses did not operate in a vacuum but in relation to other discourses about citizenship, or national identity, for example, "and a wide array of concrete social and political practices" (4–5).

A recent historical study, *Mom: The Transformation of Motherhood in Modern America,* makes an interesting point about the concept of maternalism.[11] The author, Rebecca Jo Plant, acknowledges finding the term helpful in her effort to understand how motherhood as an all-encompassing identity was reshaped after World War II into a "fundamentally private experience and a single component of a more multifaceted self."[12] Plant is attracted to the concept of maternalism precisely because it "transgresses and complicates standard political categories."[13] This is very different to the narrow images of elite "maternalist" women reformers of the early twentieth century or the related discourses of the moral mother as a symbol of the virtuous nation. Following Plant, maternalism can refer to a broad idea of gendered citizenship which may inform but not necessarily conform to certain political agendas or policy proposals.

If maternalism is defined as "social motherhood" or the application of certain "maternal" values to the society as a whole, such as the principles of nurture and care, would postmaternalism be its mirror opposite? What then would the difference be between a postmaternalist and antimaternalist perspective? Plant uses the term antimaternalism to signal a specific set of beliefs that developed in mid-twentieth-century America about motherhood becoming overly laden with political meanings and sentimentality.[14] She examines the ideas of social scientists at the time who railed against the role of mother love in American culture. Plant carefully identifies some of the complex historical processes by which moral motherhood became pathologized and discredited. In this important study, she provides a persuasive account of the absence of "mother love" in contemporary discourse in the United States.

Clearly, Rebecca Plant's analysis of the decline of social motherhood is relevant to my examination of postmaternal thinking. However, the concept of antimaternalism is of more limited use. It relies on specifically American reference points. Despite Plant's nuanced analysis, antimaternalism signals a wholehearted repudiation and hostility toward the maternal rather than a reformulation that promises liberation from old definitions and conceptions through a (purportedly) more gender-neutral stance. This promise will be critiqued in the chapters to follow. The notion of postmaternal thinking attempts to capture a development that has a broad social resonance in a range of liberal democracies. It builds on historical and policy-centered analyses, but, by bringing theories of memory into play, aims to open up new questions about the maternal and develop fresh insights into feminism and the politics of remembering.

Postmaternal thinking relies on an elaborate process of memory and forgetting. Using a concept borrowed from the prominent sociologist and contemporary theorist Richard Sennett, postmaternal thinking can be viewed as a "cultural ideal" or "cultural logic" which is linked to what he calls the "new capitalism."[15] In examining the culture of the new capitalism, Sennett argues that there is a set of cultural ideals central to the workings of neoliberal institutions, work arrangements, and conceptions of the self. Over the last decade, since the publication of his pathbreaking *The Corrosion of Character: The Personal Consequences of Work in the New Capitalism*, Sennett has endeavored in various ways to identify and pinpoint this cultural logic.[16] Certain characteristics are central to his analysis: a self oriented to the short term; a focus on potential abilities rather than past knowledge and expertise;[17] the promotion of meritocracy over craftsmanship; low loyalty; low trust; constant adaptation and fragmented life narratives. A devaluing of the principles of nurture and care could well be added to this discomforting list. As Sennett notes, these ideals stigmatize dependence in any form, including dependence on an institution, employer, or the state for support. It stands in marked contrast to the protective welfare reform championed by early maternalists. The idea of the state as beneficently striving to meet the needs of its citizens has been replaced by the individual citizen having to prove entitlement to support through signs of job readiness or "self-sufficiency."[18]

The framework elaborated by Sennett has proved particularly resonant for theorists attempting to understand how relationships, ideologies of motherhood and childhood, and the life of families have been infused with this cultural logic. Nowhere is this better explored than in the writing of Anne Manne, who draws on Sennett to develop an informed theoretical framework linking the new capitalism and the enchantment of paid work (at the expense of care) with a refashioned sense of self. Manne's work includes but is not limited to discussion of motherhood and the dominance of a particular kind of work-centered liberal feminism. She writes that the "new capitalism is profoundly reshaping our tolerance and generosity towards vulnerability. . . . Across a lifespan of childhood, adulthood, sickness, and old age, every person will be dependent and independent, reliant on others and relied upon, vulnerable and strong. Given that, we should give up our false opposition of independence and dependency, and instead talk of human interdependence."[19]

The cultural hostility to what Sennett calls the "dignity of dependence" is a key feature of postmaternal thinking.[20] I will argue that this can be seen as a kind of unmothering of society as a whole. The postmaternal therefore becomes a fantasy of self-sufficiency, the desire for sovereignty promised but never provided by market individualism. The idea of the unencumbered, self-sufficient, rational, and freely choosing agent is thus the antithesis of maternal notions of subjectivity.[21] Yet, it is the unencumbered self that most easily conforms to the instrumental rationality of the neoliberal marketplace. As Sennett concludes, and Manne reminds us, the character ideals underlying this rationality can only be realized by the very few. Iris Young expresses a similar view in a different way, arguing that the very notion of the individual as self-sufficient is a "normalizing but impossible ideal."[22] This impossibility means that there is an enduring tension between the fact of human dependency and an ideology that depicts dependence as a "failure of subjectivity."[23] The deep discomfort this produces at the level of lived experienced will be examined throughout the pages of this book.

Sennett argues that the surrender and abandonment of past knowledge is central to the workings of the new economy and its wider logic. Evidence to support these claims is not difficult to find. In organizations and institutions the cultural traits most valued are precisely those Sennett has outlined. The ability to constantly move into new roles and forget the old is valorized above all others. In the literature on global organizations this is called "planned abandonment." It is defined as being in a constant state of readiness to discard and forget previous wisdom and thus work with the forces of organizational change.[24] It is not difficult to see that, in the wake of the global financial crisis, these character traits are still being heralded as some kind of key to survival. In my view, these values are built on a postmaternal logic and have become not only the foundation for dominant cultural ideals but also a reference point for how people think about themselves. This logic, I will argue, may be culturally pervasive, but it is not always hegemonic. Later chapters will discuss resistances to postmaternal thinking. However, as a starting point, viewing the postmaternal as a cultural logic linked to the ideals Sennett identifies assists in keeping the social and political dimensions of certain forms of forgetting firmly in view.

ACTIVE FORGETTING

In an effort to move beyond policy frameworks and into different intellectual territory, the concepts of "cultural memory" and "active forgetting" will be used. The idea of memory as a cultural rather than an individual faculty gained currency in the English-speaking social sciences through the work of Paul Connerton in *How Societies Remember*.[25] While there is a long history of intellectual interest in memory, the last decade has witnessed an explosion of memory research. To some extent this has fueled or developed in parallel with the "narrative turn" in the social sciences and humanities.[26] Qualitative inquiry has been reshaped in research that focuses on the relationship between personal and public stories and individual and collective identities. While narrative research has carved out a distinct and coherent identity, memory studies remains a much more fraught area of study. Debates about the field of memory studies are varied and at times arcane. On the one hand, its interdisciplinarity is viewed as being a strength, whereas, on the other, the area is criticized for a lack of agreement or imprecision about basic concepts and methodologies. Leaving aside the details of some of these deep epistemological divisions, the concept of cultural memory provides a rich theoretical framework for an exploration of the convergence of public and private, individual and social in ideas about the maternal. The most lucid definition, and one especially suitable for my purposes, is provided by Marianne Hirsch and Valerie Smith in their introduction to a special issue on gender and cultural memory in the journal *Signs*.[27] The authors define cultural memory as the juncture of the individual and the social, where individuals and groups recall a shared past on the basis of common beliefs, conventions, and experiences.[28] However, in drawing on Hirsch and Smith, the point is not to completely bypass critiques of the idea of collective memory or ignore questions about the role of individual reminiscence. These questions arise particularly in relation to oral testimony and will be tackled later.

At the outset, the influence of Paul Connerton's more recent attempts to theorize memory need to be acknowledged as shaping the conception of cultural forgetting to be used in this book. In the inaugural issue of the innovative journal *Memory Studies*, Connerton identifies seven types of forgetting, including "repressive erasure" and "prescriptive forgetting."[29] His third type is of special relevance here. This is a forgetting that is "Constitutive in the Formation of a New Identity."[30] Connerton defines this kind of forgetting not as a loss caused by being unable to remember certain things but rather as a gain "that accrues to those who know how to discard memories that serve no practicable purpose in the management of one's identity and ongoing purposes."[31] This is quite different from popular notions of "historical amnesia," which rely more on a mechanistic and passive idea of forgetting as a process of loss or as being duped by state-sanctioned memories of the past. In my view, Connerton proposes a more interactive model; a development involving individual agency and negotiation between personal and political, public, and private memory and the social contexts in which memory-making takes place. According to Connerton, certain memories are dispensable and others desirable in the process of forming a new identity. For instance, forgetting maternal forms of subjectivity (nurture, care, and dependency) is essential to the formation of a new identity built on ideas of self-sufficiency, autonomy, rationality, and independence. There is nothing random about this process. Connerton's third form of forgetting is a patterned and collective procedure where new, shared memories and, most significantly, "shared silences" are culturally produced. Forgetting, so conceived, is a form of cultural abandonment where memories that are unsuited to changed relations of power are consigned to a "shadow world."[32] This book aims to shed some light not only on these changed power relations but also on the shadow world of human vulnerability and interconnectedness that postmaternal thinking disguises.

THE SHADOW OF ESSENTIALISM

Before introducing the structure and focus of chapters to follow, it is necessary to identify certain theoretical problems that haunt any discussion of mothering as a paradigm of social and political care. The first and perhaps the most difficult to resolve is that of essentialism. This is the view that any generalized conceptions of the maternal risk ignoring the great diversity in the lives of individual women who may or may not be mothers. Ideas that women or mothers share an essence are seen to be based on a false universal, namely, women's special or incontrovertible relationship to care and nurture. Many feminists would insist that the primary focus of the second-wave feminist movement has been one long struggle against essentialism, whether this be biological, cultural, or ideological. This makes any discussion linking women and care, or mothering and nurture, particularly troubling.

Two feminist care ethicists stand out for their bold and convincing attempts to address the issue of gendered care and essentialism. The first is Sara Ruddick, in *Maternal Thinking: Toward a Politics of Peace*, her acclaimed analysis of the distinctive forms of reasoning that are generated from maternal practice.[33] Ruddick focuses on the "cognitive and intellectual" aspects of mothering and views maternal "thinking" as a social activity with moral political and ethical dimensions. One of the notable aspects of *Maternal Thinking*, the object, subsequently, of intense commentary, is Ruddick's belief that men can engage in maternal thinking and that not only women can be mothers.[34] Maternal practice produces a different way of thinking, seeing, knowing, and acting in the world. However, Ruddick's challenge to essentialism is tempered by the acknowledgment that to use a gender-neutral term like *parenting* to describe the practices of care and nurture that shape maternal thinking would be to dishonor the "historical and cultural assignment of this work to women."[35] These contradictions are to some extent impossible to resolve. In many ways Ruddick uses these ambiguities very productively. While there cannot be a universal definition of motherhood applicable to all women, certain maternal practices, such as preservative love and fostering the growth of an infant, produce a distinctive way of thinking that can cross gender, class, and culture. The universal here does not refer to an essential womanhood identifying all women as mothers or potential mothers. Rather the universal centers on the fact of the ubiquitous vulnerability of all children. According to Ruddick, children are vulnerable no matter how privileged their social circumstances. They are "small, powerless, imperfectly made, subject to illness and abuse," and demand "what we call mothering."[36] A particular moral vantage point is not ascribed to mothers but to mothering. In my view, the shared vulnerability of children and their need for mothering is a strong universal. It resonates at both everyday and philosophical levels and challenges essentialist conceptions of women. At a broader level, it offers a different model of social relations and heralds the possibility of an alternative politics of maternalism.

Eva Feder Kittay is the other moral and political philosopher who tackles the problem of essentialism in a critical and compelling way. In *Love's Labor: Essays on Women, Equality, and Dependency*, Kittay develops what she calls the "dependency critique" of the ideal of equality.[37] Extending Ruddick's conception of maternal thinking, where preservative love is the most fundamental of all maternal requirements, Kittay emphasizes asymmetrical dependency relations. Her focus is not on

→ Olive's mother when blind.

interdependencies (where children grow up and become less dependent, for example) but rather moments when "we are simply dependent
and *cannot* reciprocate" (180). Kittay's personal narrative about her own
profoundly disabled daughter Sesha points to the limitations of liberal
notions of society as an association of "free and independent equals" (4).
Kittay advances an alternative to liberal political theory by proposing a
different claim to equality based around the fact that "we are all equally,
some mother's child" (25). This universal avoids some of the extreme
dangers of essentialism discussed previously. Similarly, Kittay presents
the inevitability of our own human dependency as another universal.
This understanding refuses essential notions of women having a special
relationship to care and nurture, implicitly acknowledging that many
women unequivocally reject both caring roles and the values associated
with care. Regardless, it seems as though Kittay is caught in the same
predicament about how to account for the thoroughly gendered nature
of the social world; namely, the reality that most caring for the vulnerable is done by women. Kittay employs a gender-neutral term, *dependency worker,* to refer to the unpaid or paid tending to others, yet she
also comments: "Nonetheless, to ignore the *fact* that most of the care
of children is done by mothers, and to call this work of caring for children parenting rather than mothering is a distortion that serves women
poorly. I therefore follow other feminists who call the care of a child
mothering, acknowledging that fathers, too, can be excellent 'mothers'"
(xiii–xiv). In the remainder of this book, I aim to follow the lead of Ruddick, Kittay, and Manne and try to work within these tensions and contradictions around gender and care. However, the problem remains difficult to solve. On the one hand, I refer to mothering and the maternal as
emblematic of a type of caring relation not confined to women alone and
with wide applicability for other social relations. On the other, the lived
bodily actuality of mothering newborns and very young babies (especially, but not necessarily, if breastfeeding is involved) tends to be experienced as profoundly "female." To empty out the category of mother
and make it disembodied feels almost as unsatisfactory as essentialist

ideas of motherhood. It risks reproducing market notions of care as a transferable commodity, further marginalizing questions about the impact different forms of care may have on those who depend on it most. Moreover, the fact that we are so cautious, if not queasy, about any hint of an essentialist connection between women and care can itself be an example postmaternal thinking. Are our fears of essentialism working to silence debate about care and justice in the social and political sphere?

In keeping with these views, I engage in an interweaving of memory studies frameworks with a feminist "ethic of care" perspective. Leaving a more detailed analysis of the strengths and limitations of care ethics to later, it is important to briefly note the influence of these ideas in what is to follow. This book aims to contribute in an original way to existing debates about care and justice. It draws on a lively body of theory which argues that ideas of rights, rules, contractual relationships, and abstract notions of justice ignore a whole dimension of moral life that revolves around care, connectedness, and a relational, "giving" conception of the self.[38] While theorists within this tradition debate the question of whether mothering is adequate as the paradigmatic mode of caring or dispute the view that a relational, connected self is more common to women, they agree that caring generates a distinctive kind of moral ethos. They also share the view that close attention to women and care throws light on a crucial and underrecognized human activity that should be shared and become the basis of alternative ideas of justice. As Kittay puts it, the issue is not whether a relational, giving self is more or less desirable, but just that it is indispensable to dependency work and the human life cycle. At no stage in this literature is the position adopted that *only* women should be the primary caregivers in society. Yet gender difference, regardless of how it may be constituted, is kept firmly in sight. This refusal of the pretense of being gender neutral is central to my argument for a commitment to a regendering of feminism. Consequently, an ethic of care approach provides a counterpoint to the cultural logic of postmaternal thinking and is a frequent reference point in what is to follow.

Marianne Hirsch and Valerie Smith remind us that "forgetting and suppression must be contested by active remembering and that the practice and analysis of cultural memory can in itself be a form of political activism."[39] This book strives toward an active practice of remembering the maternal (and maternalism) as a paradigm of nurture and care applicable to other social relations. It also remembers maternal care as an impetus for social activism. To use the words of the distinguished scholar of feminist mothering Andrea O'Reilly, the maternal can be viewed as a "transgressive model of creativity and subjectivity."[40] In stretching the concept of postmaternalism beyond its limited usage as a description of the restructuring of the welfare state, and exploring the proposition that there is a wider cultural repudiation of maternalism with profound political, social, and ethical implications, I turn to a range of rich and varied sources in a thoroughly interdisciplinary study. These include literary and historical texts, oral testimonies, online blogs, mothering advocacy sites, memoir, newspaper articles, web-based magazines, and feminist biography. This book aims to bridge the popular and scholarly divide by utilizing interpretative frameworks from sociology, political science, philosophy, feminist theory, and memory studies. It goes without saying that such an approach is by necessity highly selective. The sheer volume of material about mothering seems to proliferate daily, especially in online manifestations of maternalism. It would be impossible to adequately incorporate a representative selection of this literature here. However, I do hope I give some sense of the breadth and character of cultural expressions of anxiety around the maternal in the new and distinctive ways motherhood is being narrated. As already outlined, by viewing postmaternal thinking through the lens of memory theory I aim to shed new light on the cultural logic of neoliberalism and generate a different set of questions about feminism, memory, and politics.

The book is structured along the following lines. The project of building the foundations for a concept of postmaternal thinking is undertaken in the opening chapter. Here key concepts such as neoliberalism will be further defined and interpreted. The most recent debates about the relationship between feminism and neoliberalism will be examined alongside other elements that contribute to an *unmothering* of society as a whole. In keeping with the effort to theorize postmaternal thinking, chapter 1 will provide a more detailed analysis of Sara Ruddick's conception of maternal thinking as well as some of the "afterlives" of her influential book. The chapter will conclude by positing a connection between postmaternal thinking and the dominant ways feminism has been remembered, including, of course, political structures of forgetting that shape feminist cultural memory. Chapter 2 moves on to interrogate this link by exploring the way feminism has been represented as a movement where women were free "to give birth to themselves." Both in popular and scholarly reminiscences of the women's movement, there is a shared, collective sigh of relief at having escaped the ancient ties a mother culturally represents. A new, unencumbered (motherless) self is celebrated and defined by its separateness, autonomy, and purported freedom of choice. Detailed focus will be on the different ways feminists have remembered and written about their own mothers, concluding with a glimpse of an alternative politics where human dependency and vulnerability are imagined as the primary connection between people, not market performance.

In contrast to the second chapter's concern with the collective forgetting of the "nurturing mother" in reminiscences of feminists about their own mothers, chapter 3 focuses on questions of individual memory and whether a forgotten maternalist ethos can be detected in the early women's liberation movement. It examines a series of recorded oral testimonies that look retrospectively at mid-twentieth-century feminism. Unlike the textual accounts discussed in earlier sections, attention will be directed here to oral sources. The chapter also suggests that interpretative approaches from oral history and memory studies can work against fixed versions of feminism's history and allow more ambivalent dialogues to emerge. Chapter 4 documents the whirlwind of online activity around motherhood. It analyzes the extent to which the so-called new mothers' movement points to a reconfigured maternalism or reproduces the problems associated with the maternalism of the past. It also raises questions about maternalist impulses in popular culture as a form of resistance to postmaternal thinking. It continues by returning to Sara Ruddick's thoughtful contemplation of the epistemological connections between maternal thinking and peace often overlooked in later commentary on Ruddick's work. Forms of contemporary peace activism in the U.S. are discussed to highlight the continuing relevance of Ruddick's formulations. This section concludes with a consideration of Arlie Russell Hochschild's discussion of the troubled relationship between market and nonmarket life, particularly in shifting emotions around ideas of work, home, dependency, and care.[41] The chapter ends with a call for a different kind of feminist maternalist politics.

As will be evident, my conclusion offers some provisional reflections on the problems posed by a degendered feminism, the dominant strain of feminism in public policy debates today. Specific reference is made to the way the materiality of embodied motherhood is ignored in many policy initiatives. Progressing from where I began, with a discussion of cultural forgetting, the book ends with a form of remembering. It gives qualified consideration to some feminist responses to the current environmental crisis and suggests that the limitations of a degendered feminism can perhaps be addressed through the emergence of a theoretically informed "regendering" in new movements around feminism and environmental sustainability. In some respects, ecofeminist movements can be seen to be actively remembering the nurturing impulses of earlier maternalist campaigns. In other ways, they intersect with some of the new expressions of maternalism in current peace activism and in the online mothers' movements. While there are both problems and promises in these timely challenges to postmaternal thinking, they do signal ways forward for more open-ended dialogues about feminism and maternalism.

1

Unmothering

The world we know is one fashioned by the dreams
of those who, by and large, consider themselves independent.

EVA FEDER KITTAY, Love's Labor

Two decades ago Sara Ruddick made an observation that to claim a maternal identity was "not to make an empirical generalization but to engage in a political act."[1] Today, in stark contrast, it has become almost "politically impossible" to make a public claim on the basis of motherhood, according to feminist state theorist Ann Orloff.[2] Political support for women's caregiving role has diminished in favor of endorsing women's claims as *workers* or limiting entitlements to economically active citizens. This chapter will critically review some of the current explanations for this dramatic shift and proceed to discuss how its impact extends far beyond the policy arena to a much more widespread cultural unease with forms of nurture and care identified as maternal. Policy-oriented approaches derived from or associated with the ascendency of postmaternalism will provide a good starting point for an examination of some of the changes that have accompanied the so-called march of neoliberalism. These changes will become the backdrop for subsequent investigations of the different ways certain memories of feminism have become implicated in attempts to account for the glorification of paid work in the market over relationships involving care, nurture, and dependency.

Maternal forms of selfhood have proven especially unsuited to neo-liberalism. The shifts in social provision of the 1990s that occurred through welfare restructuring imposed especially harsh penalties on those least advantaged in our society: children, sole mothers, the frail elderly, women both in the workforce and mothers at home and poor immigrant women working in domestic labor and child care. Questions therefore are often raised about feminism's role in these damaging developments. The impressive contribution made by Ann Orloff to our understanding of the gendered implications of this restructuring has already been noted in the introduction to this book. In *States, Markets, Families: Gender, Liberalism, and Social Policy in Australia, Canada, Great Britain, and the United States*,[3] Orloff, with colleagues Julia O'Connor and Sheila Shaver, richly detail the contradictory nature of neoliberal developments in social policy in these advanced democracies. Their study encompasses cross-national variations in these four states, while maintaining a clear focus on gender relations and families. The definition of neoliberalism used by Orloff, O'Connor, and Shaver is a movement that has been strongest in English-speaking countries that emerged after 1980. The authors define neoliberalism as a reassertion of "liberal principles of freedom, market individualism and small government," where freedom is understood in the most narrow and negative sense of "minimal restriction of the individual by the powers of the state" (52). The authors' argue that a key goal of neoliberalism is to "restore market forces to areas of social life in which they had been displaced or altered by the state" (53). This restoration is achieved by transformations in the labor market including the following: increasing casualization of labor, global mobility of capital, and changing patterns of paid and unpaid work by women. Shifting gender roles and relations therefore have been crucial in decisions about restructuring the social provision of welfare support for women. Notably, such reshaping is predicated on the public recognition of a cultural transformation that accompanied women entering the labor market in steadily increasing proportions.

While Orloff, O'Connor, and Shaver highlight the significant alignment between neoliberalism and conservative political forces, they show how the celebration of market individualism is decidedly contradictory when it comes to women. On the one hand conservative opinion favors the traditional family and on the other, neoliberal policy supports the dual-earner family with care (such as child care) best outsourced to a minimally regulated market. In picturing "women in the same terms as men," as equally "possessive individuals," neoliberal policy intersects with feminist demands for freedom and autonomy, both philosophically and empirically. This has had a significant cost for women.

> Under neo-liberal conditions, the price of women's liberal individualism is that their needs and satisfactions are defined by the market paradigm. Neo-liberalism has been vocal in its opposition to welfare state support for women on the grounds of gender and gender disadvantage. It is frequently argued, for example, that intervention to address race and gender discrimination is undesirable because it contravenes individual freedom, and is moreover unnecessary because in time such problems will be overcome by the rationality of the market.
>
> (54)

Neoliberalism offers no grounds for reconciling claims for autonomy with what the authors describe as the "constraints of human dependency" (54). They collectively identify the benefits of workforce participation for women, but acknowledge that in a neoliberal context the social rewards are for paid labor, not for unpaid caregiving.

Similarly, in Orloff's penetrating reflection, "From Maternalism to Employment for All,"[4] the state is viewed as having played a significant role in translating the demands of feminist movements into material social changes. Her argument documents the shift away from maternalist policy models—which once provided for women as caregivers—to the current situation, where support is for women as paid workers via inducements, on the one hand, and coercive measures by state authorities to increase women's labor market participation, on the other. Orloff specifies what she calls a series of "farewells to maternalism" in countries ranging from Sweden to the United States and the Netherlands. Her analysis maps the different ways gendered policy regimes (supporting women to stay at home to care for children) have been "farewelled." The "abrupt and uncompromising" farewell to maternalism executed by the United States is widely known. Nowhere is this more evident than in the 1996 Personal Responsibility and Work Opportunity Reconciliation Act that replaced the social safety net for the poor with directives for welfare recipients to work and penalties if they did not. With child poverty rates in the U.S. the highest in the developed world,[5] and working mothers without paid parental leave and, moreover, with little state-funded child care or opportunities for increasing women's employment in the public sector, the maternalist state has well and truly disappeared.

It should be noted briefly that this perspective is not shared by feminist legal scholars Naomi Mezey and Cornelia Pillard. In "Against the New Maternalism" they argue that "the state, the market and the family all reinforce maternalist ideology."[6] This overstatement is not supported by evidence, particularly at the policy level. On the contrary, a hyperindividualist work-centered ideology is dominant in the U.S. and other developed industrial economies. Mezey and Pillard's position undermines an otherwise nuanced analysis of the emergence of a particular form of maternalism, detached from and conflicted in its relationship to feminism. As Orloff so carefully documents, maternalist ideology has long departed from state policy decision making. While the family and the market might present a more complicated picture, the logic of postmaternal thinking remains intact and ever prominent in cultural debates about the role of care and the implications of being dependent in our society. A further dimension is added to this argument by turning to Lynda Faye Williams's *The Constraint of Race: Legacies of White Skin Privilege in America*.[7] In her powerful study of the evolution of racialized social policy in the U.S., Williams provides perhaps the most dramatically vivid characterization of the paradoxical nature of these postmaternalist policy developments. In her view, "by the end of the Clinton years, the nation had virtually come full circle. More than at any point since the 1960s, poverty and racial discrimination, once seen as problems requiring state action, were now seen as the result of state action. What was once the solution (activist social policies) had now become the problem (dependency); and what was once the problem (the lash of poverty) has become the solution (market forces)."[8] If we take Williams's depiction here, of a world indeed turned upside down, where solutions have become problems and problems solutions, it is little wonder that in the written narratives and oral testimonies I later discuss there is such a strong perception at the personal and public level of a general failure of care, in short, of feeling unmothered.

Often the American social policy landscape that Williams describes is depicted as being at the extreme end of the spectrum. However, returning to Orloff, one can see similar policy shifts in the 1990s throughout the developed world. These changes may have been less abrupt, but their impact on those most socially disadvantaged is shown to be just as comprehensive. Orloff comments:

The U.S. approach is echoed in Europe (albeit generally in somewhat milder fashion) by so called labor market activation policies that pressure those outside the labor force—whether unemployed youths, the long-term unemployed, the disabled, older workers or mothers—to take some kind of a job. The explicitly gender-differentiated maternalist logic of politically recognizing, and financially supporting, mothers' caregiving is being displaced by ostensibly gender-neutral notions of recognizing and supporting only economically "active" adults, with support to care taking the form of temporary leaves to workers or public services for the care of their dependents.[9]

At the level of specific states, different combinations of incentives and coercions apply. The complexities of intricate forms of state provision and the distinctive ways neoliberal ideas have been shaped by national contexts and different labor movement histories are beyond the scope of this book. However, as the studies discussed make abundantly clear, there is a shared logic at work here that crosses national boundaries.

Admirably, Orloff manages to delineate features of the postmaternalist state and its new policy agenda without herself engaging in what I am calling postmaternal thinking. This is also true of her joint interventions with Shaver and O'Connor in *States, Markets, Families*. It is necessary here to return to my opening definition of postmaternal thinking as a pervasive cultural logic.[10] This denotes a situation where the values associated with maternal forms of care are repudiated in the public sphere and conflicted in the private domain. Privatizing maternal values is to deny their social significance and reduce nurture and care to the status of an individual choice. For the purposes of this chapter, this definition of postmaternal thinking can be extended to include a form of reasoning that "naturalizes" (in the wider culture) what Orloff calls postmaternalism (in the social policy arena). In the service of neoliberal policies and practices that reward if not exalt the ideals of market performance and unfettered individualism, a thinking or cultural logic which presents care, birth, interconnectedness, and dependency as infantalizing, burdensome, and somehow primitive is ideologically very useful.

Postmaternal thinking plays a key role in sustaining a normative idea of the self as both genderless and autonomous. It reinforces the dominant neoliberal claim that recognition and support should only flow to those who are economically active. It also assists in further marginalizing unpaid caregivers, thereby reinforcing unjust social relations and hiding the true gendered aspects of care. Like other ideological formations, this logic sometimes creeps into the very analyses set up to critique it. Orloff is an exception here. She acknowledges the way maternalist premises and programs were questioned by second-wave feminists as women moved into the labor force in large numbers.[11] Yet she does not forget that a significant strand of feminism was never built on the assumed equivalence between workforce participation and emancipation. This is an important point, to which I will frequently return.

Before assessing other attempts to theorize the relationship between feminism and neoliberalism, it is worth examining an instructive account of some of our deeply held beliefs about dependency. Nancy Fraser and Linda Gordon's contribution to the collection *The Subject of Care: Feminist Perspectives on Dependency* charts some major historical shifts in definitions of this term.[12] In my view their essay should be compulsory reading for anyone interested in these issues. Their genealogical approach aims to "defamiliarize taken-for-granted beliefs about dependency in order to render them susceptible to critique and to illuminate present day conflicts" (15). They are particularly successful in achieving this aim. Their starting point is the proposition that *dependency* (as a term and an idea) is a keyword in U.S. welfare discourse. The authors map the preindustrial usage of the term, highlighting that dependency was viewed as a "normal," not a "deviant condition" (17). In the seventeenth century all but the very few were dependent on someone else for their livelihood, safety, shelter, and social status. Correspondingly, dependency was perceived as a social reality rather than an individual state or condition. While it denoted a social hierarchy, it was neither a particularly gendered term—most men and women were dependent—nor did it have pejorative associations. In some respects it even had a positive meaning and was linked to being "dependable." By contrast, the term *independence* was at first only applied to aggregate entities such as the church, not to individuals. Referring to the English Civil War and the Putney Debates of 1647, Fraser and Gordon note the suspicion with which certain forms of independence were viewed. Hired help or "out-of-doors" servants, not attached to households and independently selling their labor, were seen as figures of "social disorder" (18). Fraser and Gordon's pointed inclusion of such details really does succeed in shaking up our contemporary assumptions about independence as always being a sign of autonomy, freedom, and an indisputable cultural value.

Of course, as Fraser and Gordon document, everything changed with the birth of capitalism. As wage labor became normative, those people in forms of political subjugation, bondage, or those excluded from selling their labor came to personify a form of dependency with a strong "negative charge." The authors dramatically show how the dependency of the "colonial native," the "slave," and the "pauper" was given a new moral and psychological register at this time. Gender also came into play in complicated ways, with some dependencies "shameful" in men but not so in "women." While Fraser and Gordon's genealogy of this term spans a wide historical period and carefully categorizes iconic forms of dependency in industrial and postindustrial times, it is their analysis of the strong emotive and moral connotations now attached to the idea that is of most interest here. To summarize, they show how dependency became feminized and associated with excessive emotional neediness. They also depict the ways in which dependency became defined as an individual character trait denoting a failure of will. Today, in its current increasingly individualized form, all types of dependency are considered avoidable, and all according to Fraser and Gordon are considered blameworthy. In addition, a new meaning is attached to the term, likening so-called welfare dependency and other dependencies to a form of addiction (26–27).

These shifting definitions rely on a complex process of cultural forgetting. This includes an almost complete amnesia about older meanings of dependency as normal and a forgetting of the fact that those who "stand on their own two feet" are often being propped up by a network of invisible (female) labor. Feminist interventions have long made this labor visible by revealing the support active male individuals require for full economic participation. Recent scholarship focusing on women in high-level positions in the workforce also unmasks the labor of poorly paid women who step in and perform the emotional and physical tasks required to sustain a dual-income family. More will be said on this in chapter 4. It is enough now to signal that the neoliberal, postmaternalist welfare-to-work programs and related discourses that venerate market participation for women and men are premised on keeping the "shadow world" of dependency out of sight.

If we follow Fraser and Gordon's lucid semantic mapping, it is clear that neoliberal understandings of dependence as a shameful, incomplete, and incompetence state, can be traced back to the emergent phase of capitalism. Nonetheless, in my view, neoliberal ideologies, practices, and policies have added another, equally damaging inflection to these cultural meanings of dependency. Previously, the mother-child relation was considered a "natural" dependent relationship and immune from stigmatization as a moral and psychological sign of excessive emotional immaturity or neediness. Yet the diffuse and pervasive cultural anxieties around maternal expressions of care, to be subsequently examined, demonstrate that somehow this immunity has been fatally compromised. This cultural repudiation of the maternal is so enveloping that even mothers themselves report to feeling as though they have "been returned to some primitive, shameful condition."[13]

It would seem that under neoliberal circumstances no form of dependency is immune from being experienced as disgraceful and aberrant. Ideas of the maternal as somehow a failure of subjectivity is at the heart of what I am calling postmaternal thinking. This brings us back to Richard Sennett's words, quoted in the introduction. Sennett describes the new economy as being culturally against "the dignity of dependence."[14] In his view, this is a type of cruelty to the elderly and to children who cannot survive without depending on others. It also sets up a disturbing conflict between cultural directives to be self-sufficient and the lived experience, which always involves relying on someone. Robin West, another contributor to the *Subject of Care*, perhaps provides the best description of this at the level of everyday experience. Her comments are worth quoting at length:

> Furthermore, while virtually all of us receive care for a substantial proportion of our childhood, most of us, even in liberal societies that obsessively honor and reward heroic individualism, will spend a good

part of our lives providing care to dependents, either infants, children or the aged and sometimes all three simultaneously. For many of us, this caregiving labor (and its fruits) is the central adventure of a lifetime; it is what gives life its point, provides it with meaning and returns to those who give it some measure of security and emotional sustenance. For even more of us, whether or not we *like* it and regardless of how we regard it, caregiving labor, for children and the aged, is the work we will do that creates the relationships, families and communities within which our lives are made pleasurable and connected to something larger than ourselves.[15]

ROGUE FEMINISMS

In the popular imagination, second-wave feminism is still "linked with the glorification of market work and the devaluing of family work."[16] I will argue that this memory of feminism relies on a particular kind of cultural forgetting. More specifically, it is a forgetting that renders invisible forms of feminism that have always challenged an assumed alliance between economic participation and emancipation. Failing to remember maternal feminism in turn shapes debates about a supposedly naturalized alliance between feminism and neoliberalism. Two influential essays stand out in their incisive exploration of this relationship. One, by Hester Eisenstein, depicts the connection between corporate globalization and feminism as a "dangerous liaison." Using the image of a romance, and self-consciously echoing an earlier debate about the "unhappy marriage" between Marxism and feminism, Eisenstein details the consequences of the "flirtation" between feminism and capitalism and identifies different ideological and practical uses the women's movement has served "for capitalist interests at home and abroad."[17] She traces this dalliance through a range of sites, including the abolition of welfare, the utilization of micro-credit, and, significantly, the incorporation of feminist ideas in the war on terror. The other contribution to this debate by Nancy Fraser, in many ways in dialogue with Eisenstein's, also examines the economic restructuring of the 1970s and various transformations of the international economy.[18] Fraser, unlike Eisenstein, portrays the link between feminism and neoliberalism variously as an accident of history or an unintended convergence of ideals in the service of a new form of capitalism. Agency here is not the direct responsibility of the women's movement but is located in historical forces themselves. In Fraser's schema the relationship between feminism and global capitalism is more akin to an arranged marriage. For Eisenstein it is a love union that promises to endure as long as nonmarketized alternatives continue to be delegitimized. These two important essays illuminate much about the wider political and institutional culture in which postmaternal thinking occurs.

First, in "A Dangerous Liaison? Feminism and Corporate Globalization," Eisenstein raises questions about the different ways the contemporary women's movement has "facilitated the spread and growth of corporate globalization."[19] She begins by outlining the complex interaction between the deindustrialized U.S. economy, the growth of the service sector, the so-called neo-liberal ascendancy, and the dramatic increase in women's employment that occurred since the 1970s. "Capital's strategies for increasing profitability, then, have involved deindustrialization, expansion of the service sector, and a relative shift of investment from goods production to finance. All of these developments have involved the expanded use of women's labor. As a result, the percentage of the U.S. adult female population employed outside the home rose from 34 percent in 1960 to over 60 percent today."[20] Eisenstein argues that women's increased labor force participation has in turn created a demand for replacement services (fast food, for example) and the shift toward the commercialization of care in child care, elder care, and domestic services. While this is a familiar story, Eisenstein's distinctive contribution resides in her powerful analysis of the depth and permanency of the changes unwittingly wrought by feminist activism[21] and the centrality of these changes to corporate and government strategies to maximize profit. Acknowledging the myriad strands of feminist thought and activism, including third world feminisms and socialist feminist traditions, she posits that, overwhelmingly, the dominant version of feminism has focused its energy on women's access to paid employment. The fact that in the twenty-first century it has become normative to think of women spending most of their lifetime working outside the home is put forward as testimony to the success of this strategy.[22] It is in this success that feminist efforts and neoliberal directives about a deregulated labor market coincide.

Eisenstein does not portray this coincidence as simply an unhappy convergence or an unwitting consequence of deeper historical forces, as Fraser implies.[23] While questions of agency are raised by Eisenstein, they often appear contradictory. This is hardly surprising given the complexity of the interaction between the forces under scrutiny. As the international women's movement fights for the right to participate in the market economy, it also plays a remarkably useful ideological and practical role in the promotion of marketized notions of identity. Corporations then respond by directly mobilizing these women as producers and consumers. At the global level, cheap female labor produces the profit for global capital in export processing factories in the developing world. Caring labor is also exported, and third world women work as nannies, maids, and domestics, so women in the first world can work to further generate profit. According to Eisenstein, the costs of this circuit of capital "are borne almost entirely by women."[24]

> The workings of international capital, then, systematically dismantle the structures, however inadequate, that protect women and their children—ranging from health care, education, housing, to affordable food and fuel—thus creating intensified poverty, disease, and unprecedented levels of wealth polarization. But they simultaneously invite women into the market economy, arguing that this is the path to liberation and equality . . . The legitimization of feminism masks the radical restructuring of the world economy and the glitter of

economic liberation disguises the intensification of poverty for the vast majority of women.[25]

In other work by Eisenstein, the relationship between feminist ideology and corporate globalization is portrayed as more like cooptation. Indeed, the title of her book on this topic, *Feminism Seduced: How Global Elites Use Women's Labor and Ideas to Exploit the World,*[26] implies a much more conscious exploitation or "hijacking" of feminist ideology. This is particularly clear in her blunt discussion of the way women's rights have been employed as a rallying cry for the U.S. imperial project in Iraq and Afghanistan. Here, the liberation of women is marshaled as "self-evidently part of the project of modernization and democratization."[27] Yet Eisenstein pointedly observes that the previous U.S. administration's use of feminist ideas is not just a cynical exercise. It therefore is no simple example of cooption or of agency residing with only one partner in this "dangerous liaison." Rather, she observes that there is an "important kernel of truth" in the U.S. propaganda that feminist ideas act as a cultural solvent in assisting globalization's dissolution of traditional bonds and ties between people.[28] This compelling connection between feminism and modernity means that the notion of the self-sufficient, autonomous individual is premised on being liberated from traditional obligations, most notably being freed from the constraints of care.

Feminism is one of the most important expressions of Western individualism, according to Eisenstein.[29] As such, it has played its own role in contributing to the spread of neoliberal globalization. The liaison Eisenstein thus describes can also be seen as a "farewell to maternalism," where care is viewed as a constraint and dependency a burden for the free-floating, autonomous individual. The stark depiction of this relationship is a bold attempt by Eisenstein to promote discussion of alternatives to global capitalism and, most notably, a revival of socialist feminist traditions.[30] As I have indicated, Eisenstein does acknowledge other varieties of feminist thought. Yet, in reproducing only the dominant version (no matter how self-reflexively), she risks not just "farewelling" maternalism but "forgetting" maternalist stands of feminism, which have never promoted paid work and participation in the market as the path to liberation. As Eisenstein's intervention weaves an elegant narrative of the history of the women's movement, so it engages in a form of cultural forgetting characteristic of postmaternal thinking. Remembering and viewing these elements of secondwave feminism through a different lens, through an ethic of care framework or with maternalism clearly in sight, would create an entirely different analysis of the relationship between feminism and neoliberal globalization: not an arranged or unhappy marriage but an unlikely union, doomed from the start.

Nancy Fraser takes an even more sweeping view of second-wave feminism in "Feminism, Capitalism, and the Cunning of History." Her approach is deliberately and consciously broad, and she chooses strategically to ignore the many strands of feminist thought in favor of a sweeping analysis of feminism as "an epochal social phenomenon."[31] Like Eisenstein, part of Fraser's purpose in situating the trajectory of second-wave feminism in relation to the recent history of capitalism is to rekindle theorizing around socialist feminism. Fraser plots a story of feminism around three historical moments: state-led capitalism, neoliberal globalization, and the prospects emanating from the twin events of Barack Obama's presidency and the global financial crisis. This story begins with feminism bursting forth in welfare states and excolonial development states in the postwar period. Fraser then identifies different features of state-organized capitalism and a political culture that became subject to challenge at a structural level by the New Left and emerging women's movements. Her analysis of this period focuses on feminism's expanded understanding of subordination and injustice and its systemic critique of capitalist society. While her method can at times appear overly general, she nevertheless acknowledges considerable nuance in the second-wave rejection of certain aspects of state-led capitalism (nation-state sovereignty, economism, androcentrism, and étatism). Fraser's conclusions about this period are remarkably upbeat.

In rejecting economism, the feminists of this period never doubted the centrality of distributive justice and the critique of political economy to the project of women's emancipation. Far from wanting to minimize the economic dimension of gender injustice, they sought, rather, to deepen it, by clarifying its relation with the two additional dimensions of culture and politics. Likewise, in rejecting the androcentrism of the family wage, second-wave feminists never sought simply to replace it with the two-earner family. For them, overcoming gender injustice meant ending the systematic devaluation of caregiving and the gender division of labour, both paid and unpaid. Finally, in rejecting the étatism of state-organized capitalism, second wave feminists never doubted the need for strong political institutions capable of organizing economic life in the service of justice. Far from wanting to free markets from state control, they sought rather to democratize state power, to maximize citizen participation, to strengthen accountability and to increase communication flows between state and society.

(106)

Given such extraordinary radical emancipatory promise, how then did feminism come, in Fraser's view, to "legitimate a structural transformation of capitalist society that runs directly counter to feminist visions of a just society?" (99).

Enter neoliberalism and Fraser's narrative becomes far more tentative. In agreeing that feminism and neoliberalism prospered in tandem during this second period, the question of any "perverse" affinity between them remains an open one. In Fraser's schema, neoliberalism "dramatically changed the terrain on which second-wave feminism operated" (108). Feminist ideals became resignified in the following ways. Claims for redistribution were traded for claims for recognition of identity and difference, thus promoting a one-sided culturalism. Anticapitalist critique was recuperated by the neoliberal challenge to state-organized capitalism and instead became a promotion of "the free, unencumbered, self fashioning individual" (110). Moreover, the second-wave critique of the family wage unwittingly intensified "capitalism's valorization of waged labour" (111). Fraser, like Eisenstein, wisely reminds us that this flexible spirit of neoliberal capitalism is responsible for Walmart and the *maquiladoras* (Mexican factories that manufacture or assemble products for a foreign company) as much as Silicon Valley and Google.

Our critique of the family wage now supplies a good part of the romance that invests flexible capitalism with a higher meaning and a moral point. Endowing their daily struggles with an ethical meaning, the feminist romance attracts women at both ends of the social spectrum: at one end, the female cadres of the professional middle classes, determined to crack the glass ceiling; at the other end, the female temps, part-timers, low wage service employees, domestics, sex workers, migrants, EPZ workers and microcredit borrowers, seeking not only income but material security, but also dignity, self-betterment and liberation from traditional authority, At both ends, the dream of women's emancipation is harnessed to the engine of capitalist accumulation.

(110–11)

It is important to note that Fraser does not fall into the trap of reproducing a work-centered analysis of feminism. Indeed her depiction of the liberatory potential of the early phase of the second-wave manages to bring to life an era when the promise was for structural social transformation around care as much as participation in paid labor. In this respect, Fraser engages in a form of "active remembering." In the case of the standardized way the women's movement has come to be remembered and linked in the popular imagination with the glorification of market work, Fraser makes a significant intervention. However, she stops short of identifying other templates of remembrance. The limitations of producing such an analysis of only the dominant, "liberal feminism" risks ignoring feminist critiques of neoliberalism from ethic of care theorists and Fraser's own significant work in this area. Only if the self is conceived as the abstract, gender-neutral individual of liberal universalism can feminist subjectivity be seen to resemble the free-floating, self-sufficient subject favored by the neoliberal market. I will return to this issue in more detail. Suffice it to say that such cultural forgetting works to limit discussion of alternatives to "the engine of capitalist accumulation." In failing to include other current epistemological and ethical feminist challenges, Fraser risks reproducing liberal notions of society as an association of freely choosing individuals. Ironically, this in turn closes off alternative conceptions of justice and equality, particularly concrete "connection-based ideas of equality" embedded in what Sara Ruddick has called maternal thinking. Before moving to Ruddick and her crucial significance for the arguments in this book, it is instructive to examine Fraser's attempts to resolve the dilemmas of feminism, capitalism, and "the cunning of history."

In other contexts, Fraser is distinguished for her contributions to questions about the value of care and how it should connect to other forms of social participation.[32] Her essay with Linda Gordon on ideas of dependency (discussed above) is a case in point. It is possible then that her approach in "Feminism, Capitalism, and the Cunning of History" strategically ignores some feminist challenges. However, her concluding remarks raise a different set of questions. Fraser portrays two feminisms engaged in a "disconcerting dance" with each other. One is the social movement she describes as challenging state-led capitalism and the other is its double, a discursive feminism that has "gone rogue."[33] This second version has one way or another come to be separated from its movement origins. Fraser calls on us to become more vigilant and aware of this "uncanny double" which can be mobilized for purposes contrary to feminist ideas of justice. Even acknowledging the complexities of Fraser's ambition in this contribution, her resolution feels somewhat unsatisfactory. The feral sister of the authentic feminist seems to emerge out of nowhere. She is a creation at whose feet all the charges of flirtation (with capitalism) can be laid. Not only does this appear too convenient, it fails to account for the way a social movement becomes entangled with a contradictory repertoire of concepts and definitions from popular culture and never remains in a pure original state. Fraser's formulation expresses rather than resists some of the cultural anxieties around dominant representational frameworks of feminism. In a note, Fraser suggests that Hillary Clinton and Sarah Palin could be viewed as examples of "uncanny doubles" in the 2008 U.S. presidential election.[34] Are both rogue versions of second-wave feminism, or is one the shadowy double of the other? Aside from the fact that this is an example with little resonance outside the American context, these questions highlight problems with this concluding formulation. Similarly, the promise Fraser placed in the Obama electoral victory and the potential of the financial crisis to undermine neoliberalism places feminism ultimately in a reactive role, far from the radical emancipatory force depicted in the early part of her argument. Given the explicit aim to revive a socialist feminist tradition, the conclusions to emerge are unexpectedly narrow in their political scope.

Nevertheless, the significance of Fraser and Eisenstein's determined but ultimately unresolved efforts to understand feminism's entanglement with neoliberalism should not be underestimated. Both essays simultaneously contest and reproduce dominant versions of mid-twentieth-century feminism's supposedly ultimate co-option. Both reflect and produce a distinctive cultural memory of feminism. It is at this point that a form of postmaternal thinking is in danger of creeping into their analyses. The clearly individuated "self-oriented" self of the free and rational chooser and actor, so central to the neoliberal market, lurks in the stories these authors retrospectively tell about feminism.

It is useful to point out that postmaternal thinking is not "a strange shadowy version" of maternal thinking. Fraser's idea of "uncanny doubles" does not capture the relationship between these two perspectives. Nor is postmaternalism simply an inversion of maternalist values and beliefs. In my view, the reinterpretation of the values of nurture and care that accompanied the dramatic changes associated with rising neoliberalism has involved a much more widespread cultural repudia-tion (and forgetting) of maternal forms of selfhood. The very idea that the values associated with mothering could be applied to society as a whole has lost its currency and political resonance. As I will argue, fail-ing to remember the relational, connected maternal self is to risk joining hands with neoliberalism in masking human dependency and ignoring the philosophical challenges posed by maternal thinking.

MATERNAL THINKING AND ITS AFTERLIVES

It has been two decades since the publication of Sara Ruddick's *Maternal Thinking: Toward a Politics of Peace*. These decades have witnessed the first gulf war, the invasion of Afghanistan, war in Iraq, the widespread restructuring of social provision in most developed market societies (and its negative impact on mothers and children), the expansion of cor-porate globalization, and its contraction with the current global finan-cial crisis. It would be easy to conclude from these geopolitical devel-opments that Ruddick's imaginative conception of a feminist maternal peace politics was founded on impossible ideals. However, this is not the argument to be advanced here. On the contrary, as I have already indicated, reading Ruddick twenty years on, one is struck by the con-temporary force and relevance of her arguments. For instance, while Ruddick's book influenced, and continues to shape a growing body of research into motherhood, it demonstrated none of the positivist ten-dencies evident in subsequent, conventional social science approaches to this topic. Rather, Ruddick's delicate employment of fiction, poetry, art, and literary forms of storytelling in *Maternal Thinking* prefigures the experiments in genre, voice, narrative, and interpretation that have enlivened the so-called new humanities in the last decade.[35] Similarly, her extension of maternal thought and practice to "the needs and plea-sures of any animal or plant" anticipate the recent theoretical debates in animal ethics and current challenges to our relationship with the environment.[36] The relationship between maternal thinking and eco-feminist responses to climate change will be discussed in my conclusion. However, if, as Ruddick suggests, maternal thinkers view their task as articulating "respect for unpredictable and as yet, unimagined difference,"[37] it is difficult to account for why, in a broadest sense, "the complex modes of thought and action" that constitute maternal thinking have been forgotten or overlooked at the general cultural level.

What are the distinguishing features of Ruddick's idea of maternal thinking and which features of Ruddick's conceptual framework shape my concept of postmaternal thinking? First, the centrality given to thought, both as a social activity and as dependent on practice, in this case, forms of maternal practice. Theorizing mothering as a form of "practice-based reasoning,"[38] rather than an emotional, intuitive, or physical state, and linking this reasoning to specific metaphysical attitudes, cognitive capacities, and ethical conceptions remains Ruddick's most compelling and original contribution. She describes "thinking" as both a solitary activity and as having a cooperative, public form (15). It is this latter sense of *thinking*, and this alone, that shapes my use of the term in reference to the postmaternal. It should be noted that I borrow from Ruddick the social aspects of her concept—thinking as a public form of reflection—not the philosophical reasoning underlying her connection between maternal work and thought as a distinctive discipline. This is her unique contribution to the scholarship in this area. Ruddick adopts a practicalist philosophy in her account of maternal thinking: "More important, on the practicalist view, thought does not transcend its social origins. There is no truth to be apprehended from a transcendental perspective, that is, from no perspective at all. Practicalists reject a recurrent philosophic fantasy of finding a language free of the limits of any language in which to speak of the limits of all language. Limit and perspective are intrinsic to language and to thought, not a deficiency of them" (15). The social practices of mothering and the knowledge, reasoning, and agency that result from engaging in maternal practice together shape maternal thinking. However, maternal thought is not an abstraction, but disciplined reflection, "one kind of disciplined reflection among many, each with identifying questions, methods and aims." In Ruddick's words, "maternal work itself demands that mothers think; out of this need for thoughtfulness, a distinctive discipline emerges" (24).

Much has been written about this distinctive discipline and what Ruddick identifies as responses to "a biological child in a particular social world" (17). Foregrounding the needs of children, she considers the demand for preservation (preservative love and protection), growth (or nurturance), and social acceptability as crucial universal needs.[39] My point is not to revisit these debates here. They range from discussions of the issue of cultural diversity and mothering and the normative assumptions underpinning *Maternal Thinking*[40] to critiques of a perceived lack of attention to race,[41] and differing attitudes toward institutional violence and the military among mothers of different backgrounds.[42] The general view seems to be that *Maternal Thinking* can be strikingly paradoxical in all of these areas. However, while there is an attempt to universalize the vulnerability of children and their demand for nurturance, the practicalist premises that underpin Ruddick's analysis mean that knowledge will always be partial and limited if it results from engaging in a practice.[43] In this respect, as a maternal thinker herself, Ruddick resists totalizing frameworks, emphasizing instead complexity, ambiguity, and multiplicity of options rather than "accepting the terms of a problem" (93). This is consistent with her adaptation of feminist standpoint theory to maternal practice. Among women's multiple standpoints, mothering creates a different way of seeing, knowing, and acting in the world. Importantly, Ruddick insists that a maternal standpoint and, by extension, maternal thinking is not confined only to mothers.

Patrice DiQuinzio, author of *The Impossibility of Motherhood: Feminism, Individualism, and the Problem of Mothering*, identifies this as one of the many conceptual intricacies of *Maternal Thinking*. In her view, Ruddick resists the "naturalization of mothering" because of her focus on its "cognitive and intellectual aspects" (121). Similarly, DiQuinzio argues that Ruddick resists the elements of individualism that are consistent with ideas of essential mothering.

> Ruddick's theory of mothering as a practice is implicitly an identity-based challenge to sexism and male dominance, but also to some extent resists individualism and theorizes women's difference. Understanding mothering as a practice implies that men and women are alike in that their consciousness and social relations are shaped by the practices in which they engage. It also indicates that mothering is an individually and socially significant practice in which both men and women can and should participate. In this way it undermines essential motherhood's claim that all women and only women should be mothers.
>
> (120)

Anyone therefore can and should engage in maternal practice and "develop its virtues by taking on its goals and acting to attain them" (123). If mothering produces a distinctive kind of thinking with moral, philosophical and political dimensions, then it is also an ideal that can be realized to varying degrees by women and men. Yet, as outlined in my introduction, Ruddick refuses gender neutral terms like *parenting* to describe this practice, thereby honoring the "historical and cultural assignment of this work to women" (123), and at the same time retaining the conceptual and political link between women and the maternal. To return to a memory studies framework for a moment, in preserving the maternal over more dispassionate (but often useful) formulations such as caring labor, Ruddick is engaged in her own form of "active remembering." She asserts that her reasons are in part intellectual because different kinds of caring cannot be simply combined (46–47). However, she ensures that the dynamics of gender and power are at the forefront of her analysis. In extending the terms of Carol Gilligan's pioneering work (compassion, empathy, and connectedness) to a consciously maternal idiom,[44] Ruddick reminds us of something more visceral and embodied, familiar and paradoxical. In a later rethinking of the concept of maternal thinking, one of the book's many afterlives, Sara Ruddick captures the emotional heat generated by the figure of the mother: "A hot emotional atmosphere surrounds 'the mother' whenever she appears on a feminist, academic, or political stage. Allegedly adult and public discussions become suffused with the passions of childhood: love, hate, blissful and wretched dependency; grievances no mother can assuage, longings no mother can satisfy."[45]

Perhaps one of the most potent and enduring metaphors in *Maternal Thinking* is the description of *holding* as a way of seeing and protecting with humility (78–81). *Holding* has an embodied, physical dimension, knowing when to hold on but not hold too tightly. It also has a metaphysical character, extending the discipline of preservative love beyond kinship ties to wider communities and, as will be discussed later, to the nonhuman world. To return to the debates already examined, the idea of *holding*, and its broad social significance, appears to be the antithesis of the ideals of neoliberalism. As briefly mentioned in my introduction, the central notions of "planned abandonment" in global corporate practices and Sennett's definitions of the culture of the new capitalism paint a dispiriting picture of the contemporary political and social landscape. Sennett talks of a culture demanding low levels of loyalty, constant adaptation, and fragmented life narratives. Yet, even two decades on, Ruddick's idea of *holding* as "protecting with humility" retains a contemporary relevance and offers a powerful antidote to neoliberal cultural logic. From a critical feminist standpoint, maternal thinking is intentional, thoughtful, and moral action that will "reveal the greater safety, pleasure, and justice of a world where the values of care are dominant" (135). Is it the case then, that some notion of *holding* is a key premise for any form of feminist maternalism? If we go back to Koven and Michel's definition adapted in the previous chapter, namely, the application of values associated with mothering such as care, nurturance, and morality to society as a whole,[46] Ruddick's metaphysical conception of *holding* still offers the possibility of new and different kinds of discussions about maternalism. The label *maternalist feminist* unfortunately carries with it memories of early maternalists in the U.S. and their conservative, racialized models of the family. In *Maternal Thinking* Ruddick clearly identifies the extent to which maternalism has been mobilized for narrowly nationalist causes. Nonetheless, maternal thinking as a practice and an alternative ideal promises to generate new forms of thought and action that could be considered maternalist by extending preservative love beyond the private to the public domain.

One form of remembering is to recall the fact that Ruddick's vision has lost none of its political force over the last two decades. Accordingly, this book itself can be viewed as one of the afterlives of *Maternal Thinking*. Other new incarnations appeared in 2009 to mark the twentieth anniversary of the publication of Ruddick's groundbreaking text.[47] Andrea O'Reilly, founder of the Association for Research on Mothering, now the Motherhood Initiative for Research and Community Involvement, and founding editor of Demeter Press, the first feminist press on motherhood, has edited a rich and engaging collection on different aspects of Ruddick's thought. Many contributors begin by recalling when they first read *Maternal Thinking*. They also bring to mind the enduring impact of Ruddick's work on their subsequent ideas. Descriptions of devouring the book combine with a sense of the timely nature of Ruddick's text both at a personal and public level. Patrice DiQuinzio, for instance, evokes how "becoming a mother completely remade [her] as a person." Referring to the difficulty in conceptualizing these changes, she writes: "In other words, I desperately needed Sara's analysis of mothering." [48] Others pay homage to the fact that, for the first time, serious philosophical attention was being paid to an activity central to most women's lives.[49]

At various points to follow I will refer to some of the essays in this recent collection, *Maternal Thinking: Philosophy, Politics, and Practice*. A case in point will be my discussion of maternal peace activism in chapter 4. While I see my book as a different kind of tribute to that of O'Reilly, I have nonetheless found these contributions illuminating and of real assistance in clarifying my thinking about the underlying concepts in Ruddick's work. Of great interest to those concerned with mothering and activism is the candid conversation between Ruddick and O'Reilly that opens the collection.[50] Here it is possible to gain a glimpse of the deeply reflective and self-critical nature of this kind of scholarship and to revisit in a new light some of the original concepts of Ruddick's book. However, these afterlives of *Maternal Thinking* point to a significant paradox. On the one hand, they provide ample evidence of the enduring relevance of the details of maternal thinking to feminist theory and certain forms of activism. On the other hand, there is little evidence that these ideas have been extended to society as a whole. Far from witnessing the expansion of maternal forms of subjectivity to men and to the wider society, as Ruddick so persuasively advanced, there has been a contraction of the values of care and nurturance in the public sphere, particularly in the English-speaking world. To restate Orloff's conclusions, maternalism at the policy level has been well and truly dismissed. As indicated in our discussion of this process, it is possible for women to make claims as *workers*, but illegitimate to make political claims as *mothers*.[51] The values associated with maternal care have been relegated to one of Connerton's "shadow worlds" through an elaborate process of cultural abandonment and forgetting.[52]

Repeated expressions of anxiety around the naming of certain values as maternal go far beyond individual instances of maternal ambivalence. The point here is a cultural one. It is not about mothering but rather about the way the maternal is constituted in policy debates, popular culture, personal narratives, and conceptions of desirable selfhood. Nor is this simply an argument that feminism failed motherhood. Others have done this with varying degrees of success. A different question is why feminism is *remembered* as having forgotten motherhood and whether the dominance of this cultural memory has contributed to the emergence of postmaternal thinking. At the level of individual everyday experience, it would be safe to assume that mothers and fathers tend, hold, and nurture their children with the same level of attentiveness and fiercely preservative love that has always been the case. However, the privatization of these values, and their increasing marginalization, heightens tensions around dependency and care and normalizes an impossible dream of autonomy, the dream of a self-sustaining, gender-neutral, and perpetually adult individualism.

According to Sennett, the cultural ideals and character traits dominant at the moment are an "invitation to fantasy."[53] They damage many of the people who aspire to them. If unattainable ideals of self-sufficiency are paraded as moral virtues and the incontrovertible fact of being dependent or caring for someone dependent is widely understood as infantalizing, then profound cultural anxieties necessarily ensue. Policy discussions about changes to welfare provision or analyses of state theory and neoliberal restructuring go some way to explaining these anxieties. And as this discussion illustrates, feminism is often given a key role in justifying the current dominance of work over care. In the remaining chapters of this book, my task is to raise different questions about a cultural unease with the maternal. By positing a link between postmaternal thinking and collective forgetting, my aim will be to resist the logic of unmothering and challenge the kind of world fashioned by those who consider themselves to be independent.

2

Feminist Reminiscence

Memory is crucial to the understanding of a culture precisely
because it indicates collective desires, needs, and self-definitions. We
need to ask not whether a memory is true but rather what its retelling reveals about how the past affects the present.

MARITA STURKEN, Tangled Memories

The personal memories of feminists have taken on a public and collective significance. Nowhere is this more evident than in reminiscences concerning mothering and feminism, feminist mothers
and maternal experiences. Time and again, media and popular representations reinforce the notion that feminism is responsible for women
trading maternity for market work. The testimony of young women
who blame feminism (or feminist mothers) for their decision to delay
pregnancy or their childlessness is eagerly seized upon by publishers,
bloggers, and cultural commentators in the print and electronic media.
Dismissing the emotion generated by such discussions as a backlash,
historical revisionism,[1] or as "straw feminist bashing"[2] appears all too
easy. Similarly, Nancy Fraser's formulation, discussed in the previous
chapter, of a discursive *rogue* feminism on the loose,[3] seems just as inadequate. While it is difficult to identify all the ideological stakes inherent
in various positions on this topic, it is impossible to ignore the breadth
of commentary and the emotional temperature of the debate. Both fac-
tors signal a deeply shared cultural anxiety about the maternal.

A case in point is the passionate response to the publication of Rebecca Walker's memoir *Baby Love: Choosing Motherhood After a Lifetime of Ambivalence*. Here Rebecca Walker disclosed that her feminist mother, distinguished writer and activist Alice Walker, emotionally neglected her as a child, turned her against motherhood, and officially "resigned" from being her mother just before Rebecca's first baby was born. Alice Walker apparently wrote to her daughter declaring that "she was no longer interested in the job."[4] These revelations were fiercely debated in forums ranging from *Salon*, the UK *Daily Mail*, the *Washington Post*, various online news networks, and Australian parenting sites. In a recorded interview with Rebecca Walker on National Public Radio, the interviewer, Farai Chideya, commented that Walker's experience tapped into "pretty much a non-stop conversation among people of my age, and I happen to be 38 years old."[5] This observation and the perception that such conversations are "opening the floodgates" will frame the discussion to follow.

Viewing the debate about Rebecca Walker's memories in the context of a much wider repudiation of the maternal in the social and political domain, this chapter will investigate other troubling ways in which feminists have remembered their mothers. This will include memoir, autobiography, life writing, oral history, and public discourse. It will question what in fact the retelling of stories about mothers reveals about current cultural anxieties and concerns. In discussing the different ways feminists have recalled their mothers, the point will not be the reliability of the memories represented (were their mothers really that bad?) but rather what the transmission of these memories may indicate about how feminism and the maternal are currently defined and understood. Particular focus will be on the "cultural forgetting" of the nurturing mother and the highly contradictory reworkings and responses to the second-wave feminist idea of women "giving birth to themselves."

In her compelling book *Tangled Memories: The Vietnam War, the AIDS Epidemic, and the Politics of Remembering*, Marita Sturken makes two observations crucial to my approach in this chapter: first, that memory and forgetting are mutually constitutive processes, each essential to the other's existence, and, second, that memory is a narrative, a form of interpretation, not a replica.[6] Taking these premises as given, the problem of defining "cultural" or "collective memory" remains. The terminology around collective memory that has gained currency in the memory studies field has been shaped by the influential work of sociologist Maurice Halbwachs.[7] According to his perspective, all memory is molded by the social environment and therefore is collective rather than individual. Recollections of the past are reconstructed to accord with images and ideas suited to a particular epoch. So collective memory is not just the sum of a whole lot of individual memories but formed and reformed by social, political, and intellectual forces.[8]

Feminist theorists of cultural memory have retained some sense of personal recollection by understanding cultural memory as the "juncture where the individual and the social come together."[9] In concentrating on this juncture point, I will defer the important critiques of ideas of "collective memory" and leave questions about the role of individual recollection, to the next chapter. This aside, the relationship between women and cultural memory remains a complicated one. The fact that women are often the designated keepers of family memories adds a further ingredient to the mix. Moreover, feminist practices have consistently involved the "retrieval" of women's memories in the form of stories, cultural productions, and personal testimony. So what does a feminist cultural memory that actively forgets the nurturing mother reveal and how does the ascendency of postmaternal thinking in turn shape feminist recollection?

THROUGH THE LENS OF THE SECOND WAVE

Remembering the culture of our mothers and retelling our versions of their lives has long been a feminist preoccupation. From the feminist narratives of the 1970s to the burgeoning field of women's life writing and memoir, personal memories of mothers have become the subject of intense debate. In fact, ideas about the maternal often represent the merging of the social and the individual and as such can illuminate feminist ideas of cultural memory. Moreover, feminism itself is often viewed as being a figurative mother. Perhaps the most thorough exploration of feminism as a mother figure is in Astrid Henry's *Not My Mother's Sister: Generational Conflict and Third Wave Feminism.* Henry's argument focuses on the centrality of the mother-daughter trope in debates about different waves of feminism. As I will later suggest, it reinforces the fact that increasing public significance is being given to private reminiscences, particularly where mothers are concerned.

According to Daphne de Marneffe, author of *Maternal Desire: On Children, Love, and the Inner Life,* a woman's feminism can be seen to be like a "love letter to her mother."[10] The feminist writing that is inclined to reinforce de Marneffe's ideal has different traces of the "mother-daughter plot," to borrow the title of Marianne Hirsch's feminist, psychoanalytic, and literary study,[11] to those found in the more conflicted narratives I will discuss in this chapter. A significant example of where the voice and register tend *not* to be that of the angry daughter can be found in the work of Sara Ruddick. She comments on the fact that, while she writes as a mother, what she says, and even her desire to say it, reflects her "experience as a daughter." She continues: "The protective care and careful love I received from my mother as a child seems continuous with the model of courageous and cheerful resilience she bequeaths to me now. Although I consciously write with her grandchildren and their future in mind, in remembering mothering and honoring mothers, I have taken what my mother calls 'a long walk into the past.' I now appreciate vividly the ways her work animates mine."[12] This lovingly drawn relationship between Ruddick and her mother (who was in her eighties at the time *Maternal Thinking* was written) is the subject of reflection by influential social philosopher Anne Manne in her book *Motherhood: How Should We Care for Our Children.* Manne observes something "deep in the maternal feminist tradition" that she identifies as being "a very different 'internal model,' as the psychologists call it, of *what a mother is like*."[13] She contrasts this with the mother she finds in versions of "sameness feminism;" a depressed and submissive figure, "a dependent creature so amorphous that she needs outside forces, like the structure of work, or a feminist theorist, to stiffen her spine and pull her into shape."[14] This appears to be the more dominant shape of the mothers that surface in second-wave feminist reminiscence.

When feminists recall the early days of the women's liberation movement, and remember the thoughts they had about their own mothers, it seems like anything but a loving process. A typical example is Anne Roiphe's reminiscences about her initial engagement with a feminist consciousness-raising group in the 1970s. She writes that, in respect to everyone's mothers, "we ground them up in our long conversations and spat them out."[15] Such memories, along with recollections of mothers as misguided, angry, controlling, superficial, and punishing frequently surface in the written and oral retrospective accounts of the period. The point here is not what these accounts expose about the personal biographies of the women who are doing the remembering or, for that matter, their mothers, but rather the complex political stakes and meanings involved in this kind of remembrance.

In recreating an evocative diary account of her early feminist engagement, Marianne Hirsch discusses details of her 1970s consciousness-raising group and its endless preoccupation with a range of topics, not least the group's members "own" mothers. Of the eight participants, two were women with children. Remarkably, this fact rarely became a topic of conversation or a cause for solidarity amongst participants in the group. Hirsch observes with discomfort, "neither their children nor their maternal identity ever become points of discussion among us. Instead we talk endlessly about sex and our relationship with our mothers."[16] She recalls: "Our mothers [became] the emblems of a womanhood we need[ed] to reject, and the children of our two sisters' lives do not make us any more sympathetic to the maternal project."[17] Hirsch remembers how pronounced the fear was of "becoming like our mothers," and "a maternal divide" subsequently opened up between women, with simply no ground in between. This is recorded in the essay/diary when Hirsch recalls a feminist discussion group formed over a decade later when she herself is a mother. Once again the topic of the groups' "impossible mothers" surfaced.

> The sympathy we muster for ourselves and each other *as mothers*, we cannot quite transfer to our own mothers. Although as mothers we are eager to tell our stories, as *daughters* we cannot fully listen to our mothers' stories. This tragic asymmetry between our own two voices is so pervasive as to be extremely difficult to discuss. It reveals the extent and depth of the "matrophobia" that exists not only in the culture at large, but also within feminism and within women who are mothers, ourselves who have spent a good part of our careers thinking about motherhood.[18]

For some, like Hirsch, retrospectively viewing this desire for self-definition in opposition to one's mother is an uncomfortable process and an opportunity for reflection. For others, the rejection of "their mother's values, viewpoints and voices" is depicted as absolutely essential for feminists to be able to "find themselves."[19] What women needed was not mothers or motherhood but to be free to give birth to themselves. Such memories echo a 1970 issue of *Life* magazine where Betty Rollin, a popular journalist, made an influential pronouncement: "It doesn't make sense anymore to pretend that women need babies when what they really need is themselves."[20]

Roiphe's autobiographical narrative, *A Mother's Eye,* recounts similar memories to those of Hirsch about her early encounters with feminist consciousness-raising. Of Roiphe's particular group's discussions about their mothers, she writes: "Everyone had a bitter tale to tell. Sometimes it seemed as if we were engaged in an Olympic competition to decide *whose mother was absolutely the worst.* Although we were beginning to understand the social realities that had placed our mothers on their respective shelves, we were hardly brimming over with sympathy" (19). Roiphe remembers her mother as pampered, depressed, superficial, and self-centered. Her recollections include images of her mother neglecting her children and soaking in the bath for hours with a glass of scotch balancing on the edge (5). Nonetheless, Roiphe's recollection of her mother does not represent an easy path to feminist selfhood. She readily admits to *never* having admired her mother, but also acknowledges that her mother was the person for whom her longing was greatest. "How much they need us, how crucial we are, how important is the word *mother*. How sad is the loss of a mother. How deep is the yearning for mother. This need will not go away. It is not a cultural artifact, like the male need for a wife to keep his supper warm, it is a deep implant, a hook that snares us, a connection both treacherous and wondrous" (67). This treacherous and wondrous "hook" was felt most acutely for Anne Roiphe, when she gave birth to her own children. Here, she reveals that her feminist certainties came unstuck. She recounts her shock in 1974 at Germaine Greer's suggestion in *The Female Eunuch* that children should be sent away to a commune in Italy to be raised. She records that, if someone had taken her child away from her, she would have torn her hair out, "screamed like a banshee, fought like a tiger" and wept until her "eyes fell out" (24). It is at this point in *A Mother's Eye* that Roiphe's mother is somewhat resurrected by the surprise emergence of Roiphe's own fierce maternalism. Yet memories of her mother as a "nurturing mother" never surface, even in her later ideas on why "mother love" should become central to a new feminist family politics. Memory and forgetting can be seen as coconstitutive in these kinds of recollections; the absence of the nurturing mother shapes the presence of the sad or unfulfilled one.

In Lynne Segal's feminist memoir *Making Trouble: Life and Politics*, there is an explicit acknowledgment of the way memories are constituted by present concerns; "never safe," as she declares, and always shaped by history.[21] Segal attempts to answer the question of what happens to "dangerous young radicals" as they age. She is highly critical of the way revised accounts of women's liberation have accused seventies feminists of betraying motherhood and ignoring children. Her own book makes some effort toward challenging such representations by depicting her own "backward glance" at the period. She portrays the women's movement as all about those who "tried to live with a strong sense of connectedness with and a responsibility for others" (6–7). Segal's recollections are striking and in many ways idiosyncratic, not conforming to the sanctioned version of feminist cultural memory, a point that will be developed in the next chapter. However, Segal's memories of her own mother and her mother's role in her own journey of political belonging are much more emblematic of a familiar cultural theme. She presents her mother as being crucial from the beginning, but always in a negative sense. Her particular citing of Beauvoir reveals the tenor of her memories of her mother. "As Beauvoir said, 'the great danger which threatened the infant in our culture lies in the fact that the mother to whom it is confined in all its helplessness is almost always a discontented woman.' *Discontented?* This is far too weak a word to describe my mother's bitterness and scorn reciting the litany of my father's sins" (17–18). Not that Segal depicts her father with any more affection. She describes how, in the 1960s, there were "anti-models" galore for women and few inspirational guides and mentors. Remarkably though, Segal's own mother was a long way from being the bored housewife of the fifties so frequently portrayed in popular culture. She was an admired, successful, and endlessly busy gynecologist, apparently much happier when away from her marriage, her home, and her three obedient children. Segal records that coming home was her mother's problem because "another, better world always beckoned" (25).

Like Roiphe, Segal portrays herself as a child fixated on her mother's fleeting maternal presence and feeling in some way that she somehow added to her mother's "inner emptiness." She writes: "I also saw myself as, and feel I remained, yet another disappointment in my mother's life, though I watched her in flimsy ways trying to hide it" (30). Segal also reflects on her mother's avoidance and the perception that her mother saw her daughter Lynne's crippling childhood asthma as in some way shameful. While the title of Segal's chapter, "Strictly Personal" ironically denotes the distinctive contours of her own family background, there is also a strong public dimension to these reminiscences. The meaning of the memories extend beyond the private because of a shared, public set of beliefs about how an independent feminist consciousness comes into being. Segal recognizes this and often acknowledges it in her own writing: "Even our mothers, and not only my mother, wanted our lives to be different from their own," she writes, commenting on the fact that so many of them [had] become bitter, or disenchanted, with their lot (24). At another point in Segal's narrative this intersection between personal and collective memory is made even more explicit. She retrospectively locates her individual experiences within the "spirit" of particular decades. She suggestively calls this "understanding life backwards."

I embarked upon sexual life in the Sixties, in the growing clamour for sexual liberation. I became a single mother in the Seventies, as feminism bloomed again. In the late 1980s, I began a retreat into the respectable shores of academe when, if you were lucky, you could be both paid (although increasingly poorly) and acclaimed for performing your "oppositional" politics on university lecture circuits, at just the moment when Left and feminist activism were largely vanishing from more accessible public forums, in preparation for the dismal decade of the 1990s.

(32)

The collective forgetting of the nurturing mother also features in other attempts to understand life backward. This is true of certain oral history accounts of second-wave feminism. In an interview in 2002 for the National Library of Australia, prominent Australian feminist activist and social policy analyst Eva Cox traces the origins of her feminism to her mother's bitterness and status as a victim. Cox discusses the way the breakup of her parent's marriage plunged her mother into what Cox calls "martyr mode" when her social reformer husband left to begin a relationship with pianist Hephzibah Menuhin. This martyrdom was made more significant because her daughter (Eva) was apparently deemed unworthy of her sacrifice. Cox matter-of-factly recalls her mother:

> She became a very good victim—I mean, it's one of the origins of my feminism, I think is the fact that my mother became the archetypal passive-aggressive victim type thing in the sense that the world had treated her badly, and in a way by having a daughter who was unsuccessful made her much more of a victim that having a daughter who was successful, so I think she sort of encouraged me to be difficult in a sense by constantly telling me I was like my father and I'd never do anything and I was to untidy and I was too this and I was too that and too the other.[22]

Needless to say, Cox went on to become a leading spokesperson for the Women's Electoral Lobby, the director of the New South Wales Council for Social Service from 1977–81, the adviser to the shadow spokesperson on social services in the Australian Labor Party, Don Grimes, in 1981–82, and later, academic, author, and social commentator. Like other oral reminiscences in this archive (discussed in more detail in the next chapter), the link between maternal memories and the emergence of a feminist self is consciously and directly made. Unlike a more popular narrative, namely, that the early women's liberation movement was made up of women who wanted to right the wrongs their mother's suffered, a different picture emerges from these particular retrospective accounts. Very little sympathy is expressed for these mothers. In some respects, the mode of speaking about mothers is still to "grind them up and spit them out." This is not to suggest that these women did not love their mothers or that their mothers were always unloving. Personal biographies will differ on these matters. Varying degrees of regret, grief, and longing for approval are mingled with the collective voice of the angry daughter. However, the absence of the nurturing mother in this kind of feminist reminiscence may reveal how the past has affected the present. The cultural ascendancy of what I am calling postmaternal thinking can perhaps be traced to this type of cultural forgetting. To remember the nurturing mother is to remember dependency, and this has become anathema to a particular kind of feminist selfhood.

It is striking the way individual or private memory recorded in life writing or oral testimony becomes indicative of a collective experience. Astrid Henry, in discussing differences between different generations of feminists, provides many compelling examples of the way second-wave feminist involvement was predicated on the rejection of both figurative and literal mothers: the former being represented by the first wave and the latter, women's real mothers. Henry cites Ann Snitow's proposition that "throwing off the mother's life felt like it was the only way to begin."[23] She also notes Phyllis Chesler's remarks about how politically empowering "psychological matricide" was to establishing a feminist identity. Chesler almost fondly recalls the strength of the desire at the time "to experience ourselves as motherless daughters."[24] According to Henry, this implies that "in order to bring their new movement to life—to make history, to effect change—second-wave feminists had to imagine themselves as motherless."[25] It appears then, that in mid-twentieth-century feminism, the kind of unmothering discussed in the previous chapter may indeed have been born.

REMEMBERING FEMINIST MOTHERS

One would imagine that the younger daughters of feminist mothers would have very different maternal memories. Certainly, mother-daughter language informed a particular kind of feminist commentary popularized in the 1990s and has continued into the first decade of the twenty-first century. Various authors are regularly associated with this trend, including Rebecca Walker, Rene Denfeld, and Naomi Wolf.[26] Whether or not the voices of these self-declared feminist daughters constitute a "third-wave," a term attributed to Rebecca Walker,[27] is not my concern here. There is already a broad literature on this topic. The focus is rather on the continuities and discontinuities between the different generations of feminists in respect to their cultural memories of mothers and motherhood.[28] Strangely, for feminists from a younger generation, memories of nurturing mothers continue to be subordinate to another kind of remembering. Feminist mothers are not depicted as being any more nurturing than the mothers of the early pioneers of women's liberation. According to Astrid Henry, second-wave feminism itself, in the eyes of many young women, is seen as an "embittered, puritanical mother."[29] What are the wider implications for feminism in the way that the "foremothers" of feminism are being remembered?

For the daughters of women's movement activists, mothers are often recalled as being "at the barricades" or in meetings rather than as sad victims, lying in the bath drinking gin. Yet, while prefeminist mothers are recalled as resentful, sad, and poisonous, feminist mothers of feminists fare little better. Moreover, in these memories, it is feminism that is blamed for making their mothers sad and angry. For instance, Lyn Hallstein, who describes feminism as being like her family's religion, remembers that her mother was always very clear about what she felt she personally gave up by being a mother: "Her own ambitions, sense of self, and independence. As her daughter, this was painful and confusing to me as I grew up, even though I knew my mother loved me very much. I was also always certain that my mother should and could have handled her anger better."[30] When Hallstein later gave birth to her own child and found that trying to "have it all" was nearly impossible, she recalls that her feminist mother showed little *empathy* for her situation, always reiterating that it was harder in her day and that at least her daughter could have "personal ambitions."[31]

In *Mothers and Children: Feminist Analyses and Personal Narratives*, Rachel Clift expresses similar confusion and resentment about her mother's dedication to women's issues, feeling that feminism made her mother depressed, angry, and outspoken. Clift remembers as a child trying to imagine the women's conferences her mother frequently attended as "a place where my mother and her friends would sit in a circle and discuss how they had been mistreated."[32] Ironically, perhaps, Clift's reconciliation with these memories came about when, as an adult, she encountered the writings of other feminists.

There is a pattern in such recollections that transforms them from private testimonies to collective records. Dialogues between daughters of a younger generation and their memories of feminist mothers have taken on a wide public significance. A case in point is the "why weren't we told story," which accuses feminist mothers of giving their daughters the sense that motherhood was secondary to pursuing a career or self-fulfillment, until sometimes it was "too late" to become pregnant. In *Baby Love* Rebecca Walker describes her impression that childless daughters were all around her, like some "macabre human version of dying on the vine."[33]

> We learned that children were not to be pursued at the expense of anything else. A graduate degree in economics, for example, or a life of renunciation devoted to a Hindu mystic. To live life as one long series of adventures in "sexual freedom" could be added to the list, along with becoming president, or at least secretary of state.
>
> I don't remember exactly how these ideas were transmitted, but that I imbibed them is unquestionable. It must have had something to do with my mother being a cultural icon, and the private carryover of her public insistence that even one child could, if not managed properly, erode one's hard won independence.[34]

Walker doesn't remember how these ideas were conveyed. Other women of her generation also comment on having no recollection of their feminist mothers telling them what was positive about being a mother. Interestingly, this appears to be a cultural memory based on amnesia, the *not* remembering mothers who presented motherhood as in any respects valuable and important. In the Australian context, journalist Virginia Haussegger sparked a wide public debate by discussing the way daughters of feminists had been misled by their mother's purported belief that "having it all" was possible. She discussed infertility as often being a direct result of women delaying pregnancy because of a lack of nurturing advice from their mothers. Haussegger called this "the sins of our feminist mothers."[35] Her article with this title, which later became the basis of her book *Wonder Woman: The Myth of Having It All,* generated lengthy and heated arguments in a range of national media. "I am childless and I am angry," Haussegger cried, describing how foolish she felt for taking "the word of my feminist mothers as gospel."[36]

It is important to situate the public commentary informing these pronouncements within a body of writing that first gained prominence at the beginning of the millennium. This commentary, like the interventions of the so-called third wave that preceded it, is almost entirely dominated by the voice of professional, privileged women. Working-class voices are absent from these narratives. Examples include Naomi Wolf's *Misconceptions: Truth, Lies, and the Unexpected on the Journey to Motherhood* and Danielle Crittenden's *What Our Mother's Didn't Tell Us: Why Happiness Eludes the Modern Woman.*[37] Notably, the titles signal a deliberate deception on the part of real or figurative mothers. In the view of Carisa Showden, this mother-daughter language serves to depoliticize feminism. The idea that we are witnessing the "daughter's rebellion" is neither politically viable nor "theoretically accurate," according to Showden.[38] Similar observations are made by Jonathan Dean, who concludes that such debates are reductive and misrepresent current feminism as merely a site of intergenerational conflict.[39]

If cultural memory is to be viewed as a narrative, not necessarily as reliable recollection, then it follows that the way mothers are remembered will be open to dispute. Indeed, Susan Douglas and Meredith Michaels parody the bad advice or "why weren't we told" scenario, arguing that they simply have no memory of mothers of twenty- to thirty-year-old daughters saying "Honey, I definitely do not want grandchildren. I want you to get that promotion and work seventy hours a week instead of sixty."[40] Others more cautiously dismiss the widespread cultural anger directed at feminist mothers. In *The Great Feminist Denial,* Monica Dux and Zora Simic provide countless examples that the targets of the blaming feminism discourse are made of straw. In their view, many media debates concerning feminism and motherhood perpetuate a misleading image of "motherhood in crisis."[41] While they argue that "feminism is not to blame for leaving us with a world where motherhood and work and all the other bits in between refuse to fit seamlessly together," they also acknowledge that feminism is "part of the story."[42] However, their book, with its attempts at humor (how feminism ate my babies), tends to downplay the broader cultural issues at the heart of the disquiet expressed by the likes of Haussegger, Wolf, or Walker or the fervent responses to this issue in newspapers' letters pages or in online forums. In my view, this risks ignoring the genuine and widespread cultural anxieties that have surfaced and intensified around the maternal. The fact remains that there is a palpable anger in the why weren't we told narrative that may signal concerns beyond the bad advice of individual feminist mothers.

Another interpretation of this narrative is offered by Natasha Campo in her analysis of popular culture, *From Superwomen to Domestic Goddesses: The Rise and Fall of Feminism.* This approach also displays similar limitations. Campo attempts to define a "feminism failed me discourse" and assess its impact on public debate in Australia and abroad. She identifies changes to established "memory narratives" of feminism and links them to the political culture and social policy shifts of the 1990s.[43] Many of the examples she supplies from media debates are similar to those discussed by Dux and Simic. Before highlighting some of the problems with Campo's formulations, it should be noted that, while her focus is on the way feminism has been represented and remembered, there are significant differences between her approach to memory and my own. Campo refers to the fact that her aim is not to determine whether certain memories of feminism are true or false but rather how meaning has been shaped in the popular media.[44] Campo is then selective in the media commentary she chooses to discuss in any detail. Moreover, she depicts some writers as "conservative," largely anyone who resists valorizing paid work, and others as "brave," namely, those who celebrated paid employment as the source of social identity.[45] This classification and the language used to convey these differences implicitly serves to make a judgment about certain memories being more true than others. It reproduces the divisive politics of the so-called mother wars and the tired accounting characteristic of the work/family balance debate. It is also based on a fundamental misrepresentation.

For instance, Campo's inaccurate description of social philosopher Anne Manne as a "conservative journalist" is combined with another, more direct and troubling misreading of Manne's work.[46] It is a misreading that cannot simply be explained by poor scholarship. Campo writes that, for Manne, motherhood "was not a 'role' that could be formed by either sex or by any adult. It was an instinct, something only women had."[47] Notably, this is not Manne's position. In fact, the attachment theory Manne uses in *Motherhood: How Should We Care for Our Children* is antithetical to ideas about mothers having biologically based instincts. Manne clearly documents examples where fathers would have been better caregivers than mothers and also advocates integrating attachment models into child care.[48] In discussing the economic and social penalties imposed on those giving care, she shows how men engaged in sustained caring work, such as stay-at-home fathers or sons looking after elderly parents, suffer similar stigmas to women and also have to contend with work-centered notions of masculinity. Moreover, her recommendations for radical policy changes around reduced working hours, extended parental leave, increased pay for child care workers and universal access to preschool are not founded on, or linked to, an idea of "maternal instinct."[49] Manne's writing does not impose a single, normative standard on women. As such it represents a thoroughly feminist intervention.

In *From Superwomen,* any view that challenges dominant neoliberal frameworks is presented as either media distortions of the true emancipatory nature of second-wave feminism or an unspoken alliance between a group of women journalists and the right-wing government of the time. There is an almost complete failure to account for the strength of feeling mobilized by bringing the needs of children into public view. This is not a radical position. It is as though any move away from a work-centred and neoliberal perspective on subjectivity threatens to destabilize a very fragile consensus about what is considered meaningful and what is deemed a worthy contribution to society.

By contrast, Lynne Segal manages to reject representations of feminism as antichild or antimother without endorsing neoliberal valorizations of paid work or institutional child care. She provides different evidence of what she considers to be a form of historical revisionism, a repackaging of feminism. In her memoir of feminist and community activism, Segal reminds us that many of the campaigns in the 1970s were directly around issues of providing support for mothers and children.[50] Her version of the past very much reflects the history of British and Australian welfare-state struggles for services for women. By contrast, more individualist, market-oriented feminist agendas are evident in American perspectives, as indicated in the previous chapter and in the perspectives of the "feminist daughters" discussed here.

In some respects the repudiation of the mother associated with second-wave feminism is indeed linked to recollections of paid work as the path toward emancipation and away from the mother. Daphne de Marneffe, for instance, portrays women's working life as a way of surpassing or vindicating her mother's life and feeling "truly independent." In her words, this is perceived as becoming "mercifully freed from the ancient mother-daughter cycle."[51] According to this narrative, paid work and giving birth to the (motherless) self are thus intimately linked. Once again, there is an intersection between the logic of neoliberal policy around work and feminist demands for autonomy. This illusion of self-sufficiency and the related fantasy of motherlessness is a key feature of postmaternal thinking.

The process of memory and forgetting around feminist mothers heralds the birth of a particularly modern, unencumbered self. In the type of memoirs and reminiscences discussed so far, there is a shared, collective sigh of relief at having escaped from the ancient ties that a mother culturally represents. Actively forgetting the nurturing mother thereby smooths the transition for a new self —defined by its separateness— to come into being. This unfettered self reinforces the current dominant social meanings of care and dependency. Care-related activities are represented as a burden, and dependency is somehow shameful. Moreover, obligation or duty is not only viewed as oppressive but also as infantilizing. Jean Bethke Elshtain evocatively calls this the "ultra-liberal" self. Its power in the current period ensures that women's lingering links to birth and nurturing are viewed as only "the vestiges of our pre-enlightened history and origins."[52] Purged of these relics, the ideology of this new selfhood is the freedom to choose the connections one makes to others, ahead of ties of birth and tradition. This self can also be viewed as a postmaternal self, paradoxically ungendered and thoroughly instilled with the market ideal that it is possible to be the "owner" of one's own person.[53]

According to theorist of democracy Monique Lanoix, the concept of the liberal citizen is also based on an idealized model of a permanently competent, genderless adult who must possess all the requisite capacities for self-government. Lanoix argues that one characteristic often uncritically accepted about this ideal of the citizen is that it requires a person to be fully competent "over a complete life, thus a perpetual adult."[54] In this respect the citizen is ageless. In keeping with postmaternal thinking, human dependency is yet again masked by such conceptions. As indicated in the previous chapter, critics of neoliberalism such as Richard Sennett provide striking evidence of how people think of themselves in relation to this requirement for perpetual self-government.

He argues that a new character ideal has developed in response to the impact of neoliberal restructuring of work arrangements. This new ideal is typified by the figure of the consultant: freelance, able to become an expert in any field, capable of constant self-reinvention, and dependent on no one. Ironically, the attraction of this ideal is that it can be experienced as being more democratic. "It is an ideal that is seen to be about what is *in* you, rather than how much money you have," according to Sennett.[55] Yet, to expect an elderly person to behave like a consultant or stockbroker is, in Sennett's vivid words, "a cruelty."[56] It is not surprising that the neoliberal dishonoring of dependency is also predicated on such a denial of aging.

Communitarians and feminist sociologists have attempted to critique these conceptions of the self and prevailing cultural understandings of care and dependency. Arlie Russell Hochschild, for instance, identifies a "care deficit" in contemporary society where care is produced less and less and consumed more. Care is outsourced to others or measured by buying the right service or thing. The anxieties around this marketization of emotional labor will be discussed in chapter 4. Hochschild demonstrates how principles of efficiency, once confined to the workplace, have increasingly permeated nurturing activities to the extent that home can seem more like "work" than work.[57] This care gap is given a global dimension in Hochschild and Barbara Ehrenreich's edited collection *Global Woman: Nannies, Maids, and Sex Workers in the New Economy*. Here the authors highlight the ways that the First World maintains its lifestyle by a global transfer of emotional services associated with a woman's traditional role—child care, homemaking, and sex—from poor countries to rich ones. "It is as if the wealthy parts of the world are running short on precious emotional and sexual resources and have had to turn to poor ones for fresh supplies," they contend.[58] The question remains whether the repudiation of maternalism and the cultural forgetting of the nurturing mother are also linked to this perception of a care scarcity.

Other communitarians such as Amitai Etzioni take a less international perspective and blame the care deficit on parents themselves. He argues that parents have "flown the coop" in contemporary American families.[59] The so-called empty nest is not children leaving home but parents investing so much time and energy in work outside the home that they fail in their moral commitments to their children. Etzioni's form of communitarianism emphasizes moral and personal responsibility and contrasts with the issues raised by left communitarians, such as inequality and the way governments and businesses cut communal services and work conditions. According to this perspective, the ability of families and communities to adequately fulfill their caring responsibilities is undermined in neoliberal societies. Both approaches consistently pose metaethical questions about the role of care in contemporary society.

Overlaps exist between the feminist ethic of care tradition and some forms of communitarian thinking. For example, Johanna Brenner and Janice Haaken praise communitarianism for pointing out the poverty of bourgeois individualism, "insisting that humans are constituted through a web of relational, intergenerational experiences and obligations that form family and group life."[60] Jean Bethke Elshtain's work is another example of gendered arguments situated within a communitarian framework. She contends that hegemonic forms of extreme individualism produce a thin self, emblematic of what she calls the "unbearable lightness of (contemporary) liberalism."[61] Consequently, we become tourists of our own lives, drifting from one experience to the next like sightseers. By comparison, embedded, generative activities frequently performed by women (care for children, the sick, and the frail elderly) are often based on deep unchosen ties. These ties, she argues, give weight and meaning to a relational self, defined by its connection to others. In contemporary narratives about becoming a mother for the first time, this embedded self is often experienced as being alien and dislocating. A longing for a child-free "thin" self is expressed. Take, for example, Rachel Cusk's observations about going out into the public world with her new baby. "Because I am the baby's home, there is nowhere I can leave her, and soon I begin to look at those who walk around me as *light* and *free* and unencumbered as if they were members of a different species."[62] In recording these feelings, Cusk possibly demonstrates that for young women brought up to feel genderless it is the weightiness of connectedness that is considered "unbearable," not the lightness of being to which Elshtain refers.

The gendered nature of deep unchosen affective ties has long been debated in feminist care theory. Views range from those depicting relationships of obligation as premodern, the product of exploitative power relations, to other perspectives where caring roles represent a specific attitude of moral attentiveness.[63] Care ethicists argue that such attentiveness should be universalised in order to create a more just and equal society. Eva Feder Kittay offers perhaps the most thoroughgoing critique of the neoliberal self and, by association, what I am calling postmaternal thinking. In her discussion of the relationship between care and justice, she argues that "we are connected through our own vulnerability when dependent and our vulnerability when caring for dependents, as well as through the potential of each of us to become dependent and to have the responsibility for a dependent. The bonds that form through relationships of dependency are frequently deep and count among those we most cherish."[64] Kittay is critical of the limitations inherent in the communitarian approach and, by implication, challenges some branches of feminist care theory. She points to two related and problematic assumptions at the heart of this platform. First, the model of care based on the parent-child relationship and, second, the link between a revaluing of care and ideas of reciprocity. According to Kittay, both assumptions view care-related activities in terms of their "use value." They remain outcome oriented, valuing care solely because of its instrumental benefit to society. Given that children are temporarily dependent and eventually become capable of reciprocity, their care should not, as Kittay argues, become the paradigm for a new ethics to create a more just, equal, and compassionate society. Kittay goes a step further than many feminist theorists. The key to her argument lies in her conception of the vulnerability that connects people to each other and in her rejection of neoliberal doctrines. Using the care of the terminally ill or those severely disabled as an alternative paradigm, Kittay contends that any society that is morally decent "understands that fully dependent persons must be cared for irrespective of their productive potential" (534). The sense of equality she wants to promote is based on the responsibility to provide care, even if the cared-for is never able to reciprocate (536). "It is not a hypothetical imperative; it is a categorical imperative. It is not something we must do only given that we desire some better outcome—for example, that we can assure that we raise a child to become a productive citizen or that we will restore an ill or disabled person to productivity. The dignity of persons as ends-in-themselves mandates this moral imperative" (534–35). The conception of equality here could not be further from the one that is recorded in the cultural memory of the feminist movement. The embedded, relational, and weighty self advanced by ethicists like Kittay is constituted through an infinite spiral of relationships that reaches both into our pasts and projects into future generations. She calls on us to remember that we are all equal in one sense, that is, "we are all some mother's child" (536). This is precisely what has been actively forgotten in the dominant memory of feminist eagerness to give birth to a motherless self.

COUNTERMEMORIES

In "Seven Types of Forgetting," Paul Connerton introduces a kind of forgetting that assists in the formation of a new identity. For the purposes of understanding postmaternal thinking, this type proves to be the most relevant. Connerton views it as a forgetting that rewards those who "know how to discard memories" which no longer serve a practicable purpose.[65] He uses the metaphor of a jigsaw puzzle to explain how some memories are "like pieces of an old jigsaw puzzle that if retained would prevent a new jigsaw from fitting together properly. What is allowed to be forgotten provides living space for present projects."[66] The patterned and collective process of forgetting of the nurturing mother and human dependency could well be described in this way. However, as I have indicated, cultural forgetting is always an impartial and contradictory process and never only experienced as a "gain that accrues." There are always resistances to prevailing cultural logics and, as such, postmaternal thinking is widespread but not a hegemonic system of thought.

Forgotten memories of being dependent and embedded in a web of human relationships, for instance, are often described as resurfacing when feminist women literally give birth to and nurture children. Anne Roiphe, who was cited at the beginning of this chapter as remembering the bitter Olympic competitions about whose mother was the worst in feminist consciousness-raising groups, is caught off guard when she gives birth to her first child: "I was in love with my child, not sanely, not calmly, not rationally but wholly and completely, the way people get on an airplane and give control to the pilot, to the currents of wind and let themselves be lifted up, taken away. It is indecent both in its proportions and in its motives. Deep [sic] embedded in this love was the story of my life, both the past and the future, my handprint on the universe, so to speak."[67] Continuing a dialogue across generations, Anne's daughter, Katie Roiphe, the author of *The Morning After: Fear, Sex, and Feminism,* created a storm of online protest when she described her wild love for her new baby as being "like a narcotic."[68] The debate provoked by this declaration of maternal love will be discussed in chapter 4. It is enough to point out here that the mother-daughter language used by Katie Roiphe persists by recalling the "minor dishonesties of the feminist movement" as downplaying the passionate emotions of motherhood.

Others write about a similar intemperance when it comes to maternal love. Shirley Garner writes about becoming like a country without borders after having her own children. Far from experiencing the self as separate and autonomous, she felt "newly permeable, taken over in a way [she] had never experienced." Garner recalls her two tiny children fighting over who would sit on her lap: "Their thinking of me as "the lap" depended on some continuity they felt between their bodies and mine. My body was theirs. I was theirs. To some extent, I am *still* theirs."[69]

How do we reconcile such sentiments with the desire for the impermeable, sovereign self (borders intact) recorded in other feminist recollections? The unresolvable tension here is perhaps another social and political consequence of postmaternal thinking and the active forgetting of the nurturing mother. If the motherworld is re-remembered when women become (or fail to become) mothers, as in the case of the memories discussed in this chapter, then feminist subjectivity will always be conflicted and in dispute with the demands of neoliberalism. Patrice DiQuinzio sees feminism having "only paradoxes to offer as a result of its conflicted relationship to—its simultaneous reliance on and challenge to—individualism."[70] The cost for women who identify themselves with feminism is therefore to live with contradictions that go to the heart of the very conceptions of self.

These contradictions are most evident in the maternal confessional writing that emerged at the turn of this century.[71] As I have indicated, these memoirs represent the perspectives of privileged, middle-class, young women. In some cases, it is the self-professed daughters of feminism who record their subjective experience of birth and mothering. In others, the figure of twentieth-century feminist activism lurks like a shadow in the discord between private maternal identities and the public world of work. Most of this writing describes a crisis of selfhood alongside a sense of shock about not being immediately in control and proficient at caring for a new baby. Naomi Wolf records her own sense of dislocation on becoming a mother and the grief of other new mothers in her social circle.

> You have a new baby, what you get is the whole world filled with gifts but also with losses. While the gifts new mothers receive are well documented, the losses are often hidden. This is one truth we are not told . . . Although a child and new love have been born, something else within the new mothers I heard from had passed away and the

experience was made harder because the women were, on some level, underneath their joy in their babies, quietly mourning for some part of their earlier selves.[72]

Others directly contrast their prematernal ability to approach professional demands and obligations with an unshaken confidence and competence. Susan Johnson, in her extraordinary memoir *A Better Woman*, describes her belief that she was captain of her ship, mistress of all she surveyed until having a child. She fully embraced the feminist message "It's my body, it's my life."[73] Johnson recalls that at forty years old, before her pregnancy, she had harbored no thwarted wishes, no sense that life had ever said *no* to her.[74] Unlike some of the memoirs in this genre, the remarkable privilege and hubris of this position is fully acknowledged by Johnson.

Ruth Quiney's "Confessions of the New Capitalist Mother: Twenty-first-Century Writing on Motherhood as Trauma" provides the best elucidation of these confessional narratives that present maternity as a traumatic loss of self. Through detailed textual readings, Quiney highlights the way maternity is depicted "as acutely threatening to clean individuation" and a profound crisis in identity.[75] In concentrating on the work of authors like Rachel Cusk and Naomi Wolf, she articulates the deeply contested cultural space from which these maternal memoirs emerge. Cusk, for example, describes birth not only as "that which divides women from men" but also as that which "divides women from themselves, so that a women's understanding of what it is to exist is profoundly changed."[76] Quiney contrasts these narratives with earlier second-wave feminist explorations of motherhood by Adrienne Rich and Phyllis Chesler, which, while expressing some of the same contradictory emotions, were born from a hopeful, collective, social movement, with its promise of new forms of identity.

Conversely, maternal confessional writing of the last decade represents the struggle to superimpose the old neoliberal (or ultraliberal) self onto a new and far less publicly valued maternal identity. Quiney details the way motherhood is depicted as "a curious and urgent mixture of career (with its own regimes of training, information and on-the-job surveillance) and sacrificial moral vocation. It is treated as a discipline, a brutally detailed regime of self-surveillance and professional advice."[77] The so-called new capitalist mother experiences the relationships of nurture and care as unprofitable, unproductive, and in some senses a primitive, shameful condition. To compensate, ideas of productivity are projected onto mothering. In reading the examples Quiney documents alongside other writing in this genre, clothes seem to feature as a particular kind of signifier of loss of a proficient public identity. Both Wolf and Cusk describe in visceral detail their disgust and demoralization at the "baby stains" on their clothes, in cars, and in their kitchens. These stains somehow further plummet the self into a more primitive state. Interestingly, this lower state is also represented as gendered, as though *before* becoming mothers these women experienced themselves as genderless beings. The shock of this recognition is a feature of this writing and once again contrasts with the earlier work of Rich and Chesler, who self-consciously write from a thoroughly gendered subject position. This "surprise" discovery of a gendered self is viscerally described by Wolf: "I felt as if I had fallen into a primordial soup of femaleness, of undifferentiated, post-fecundity."[78]

Despite the fact that there is a popular satirical branch of this kind writing,[79] the memoirs discussed here starkly present a genuine and often tortured struggle to make public the privatization of nurture and care and its personal and social consequences. While highly contradictory and at times paradoxical, the writings nevertheless succeed in articulating significant cultural anxieties around maternal subjectivity. The difficulties embarking on such an enterprise are witnessed in the various observations about feeling silenced by mothering. Cusk depicts her experience as somehow inexpressible. "When I became a mother I found myself for the first time in my life without a language, without any way of translating the sounds I made into something other people would understand."[80] Johnson also writes about finding herself "rendered dumb" by the bodily experiences of pregnancy and birth: "Any sense I had of being in complete control of my life (and by extension my body) was about to be challenged, and my old concept of myself smashed and made anew. Life was giving the orders now, and I had been effectively rendered dumb. Sitting there, I felt impotent and liberated, at once."[81] If the maternal self is unspeakable, it is nonetheless writable and comes into being in these memoirs. Perhaps an explanation of why motherhood is represented as such a "cataclysmic crisis" is that the cultural directives governing our sense of value have become so thoroughly postmaternal. If making a claim on the basis of motherhood has become politically impossible, to reuse Orloff's words, and support for women as caregivers has diminished, it follows that the personal anxieties of mothers would increase. These anxieties reveal cracks and fissures in postmaternalism as an ideology informing social policy and as a wider cultural repudiation of nurture and care.[82]

In recalling and recording these experiences of birth and motherhood, the young feminists writing about contemporary maternal subjectivity are producing countermemories, in the sense of providing alternative narratives that defy and so attempt to transform official historical accounts. It would be tempting to conclude overall that in the mutually constitutive processes of recall and forgetting shaping feminist cultural memory, the embedded, care-oriented motherworld has been completely left behind. In this respect, women become like immigrants. "Like immigrants moving from country to city, many women have emigrated from the cultures of our mothers to that of our fathers. But what of the language and love of that old mother culture, imperfect as it was, have we been able to keep and share with men? What have we left behind? Does what we have feel right? On what basis do we tell?"[83] While some may portray this journey as akin to a one-way adventure with little hope of return, feminist ethicists like Kittay remind us that this is not the only path we can follow. Remembering human interdependency in all its weightiness and fragility promises a different kind of politics, as many maternalist and child-centered feminists have pointed out.[84] Anne Manne calls this the "moral terrain of the connected self," a place where the ethical imperative to care for another transcends the claims to the self.[85] Remembering the embedded self may promote alternative definitions of equality that do not reproduce the care deficit or weak ties so crucial to the culture of neoliberalism. What a culture chooses to remember and forget has a decidedly political character. In the deep discomfort surrounding the maternal in feminist reminiscence, it is possible to see a glimpse of an alternative politics where human dependency and vulnerability are imagined as the primary connection between people, not market performance.

3

Memory and Modernity

"The difficulty with celebrating modernity," he declared,
"is that we live with so many persistently unmodern things.
Dreams, love, babies, illness. Memory. Death. And all the natural
things. Leaves, birds, ocean, animals. Think of your Australian
kangaroo," he added. "The kangaroo is truly unmodern."

GAIL JONES, Dreams of Speaking

In contemporary narratives documenting the experience of early
motherhood, women describe feeling as though they had been
returned to an ancient time, to a "primitive, shameful condition"
where they find themselves without language and drowning in a "primordial soup of femaleness."[1] The maternal is rendered as persistently
unmodern. Similarly, in narratives marking the success of second-wave
feminism, the rejection of maternalism is a key ingredient. This rejection is also the sign of a particularly modern form of selfhood. The historical connection between ideas of female citizenship and maternity,
in the form of policy support for the needs of mothers and children as
child endowment and welfare provision or in political claims based on
motherhood, are all things of the past, according to the logic of postmaternal thinking. Earlier chapters have attempted to highlight some
of the characteristics and consequences of this kind of thinking and
to link the cultural ascendency of postmaternalism with complicated
processes of memory and forgetting. As I have argued, different theoretical frameworks are required to understand the various ways memories of feminism have been mobilized in support for or in opposition to

neoliberalism. In public discourse these memories have also been used to explain cultural anxieties around motherhood and a widespread discomfort around the experience of dependency and care. Maternalism has in effect been privatized, with the market increasingly taking on a primary role. While this shift has been consistent with and fundamental to neoliberal economic and social principles, the blame is often ascribed to either the achievements or the successes of the feminist movement.

The preceding chapter concerned collective memory. It focused on the metaphorical matricide of early feminists and went on to discuss more recent maternal recollections by the so-called daughters of feminism. The accusation by these daughters that feminism, and their own mothers, inculcated them with the view that career came before motherhood was explored. Questions remain, however, about whether the memories of second-wave feminists themselves confirm this view. Do those key participants or pioneers of the women's liberation movement of the 1960s and 1970s retrospectively view their activism as being driven by a desire for stellar career success or professional recognition? To what extent is the dominant public discourse reflective or productive of ideas repudiating the maternal? This chapter will address these questions by examining a series of oral testimonies looking back at mid-twentieth-century feminism. It will shift attention away from the textual accounts discussed in the previous chapters to oral sources and suggest that interpretative approaches from oral history and memory studies can work against fixed versions of feminism's history and allow more ambivalent dialogues to emerge. These dialogues challenge some of the dominant public memories of second-wave feminism and reveal a maternalist ethos that has been overlooked in the way much of feminism has been remembered.

Shifting the focus to oral narratives raises certain methodological questions about "voice" and memory. The voice of feminists looking back and remembering the women's movement in oral history provides a richly dialogical site for the investigation of cultural memory. However, in what follows, the point will not be to reproduce ideas of voice so central to the conventional social sciences. Certainly, feminist oral history has been shaped by debates about the radical potential of allowing women to "speak-for-themselves."[2] This notion of voice has an almost iconic status in feminist and social science research. Engaged researchers have long struggled to find different ways to give voice to the voiceless. A cornerstone of feminist emancipatory research has been the recovery and privileging of the authentic voice "that speaks of material, historically subjugated experiences."[3] Yet, any brief excursion into contemporary, conventional attempts to give voice to maternal experience—through fieldwork-based research, interviews, and focus groups—is often disappointing by its failure to move beyond popular media representations and public discourses about the work/family divide or the unbridgeable gulf between feminism and motherhood. This is not to say that such voices are inauthentic. Any investigation of the maternal is already situated in contested and ideological terrain. However, experiments in genre, voice, narrative that have informed new modes of social inquiry, including oral history, may offer different possibilities.

More nuanced conceptions of voice are being formulated by contemporary oral historians and theorists of oral history. In "I'm a Keeper of Information: History, Telling and Voice," Rhonda Y. Williams develops a notion of voice as being more than the spoken words in narrative but also "how those words are performed."[4] According to this conception, Williams sees "close listening" as a way of unveiling the atmosphere of an interview and gaining insight into the process of reconstructing social reality. In keeping with this approach, the past is reconstituted through the oral history interview in a dramatic and more contingent way. In my view, this contingency opens the space for discourses which can challenge dominant representational frameworks. This chapter will engage in a form of close listening to a series of oral history interviews of prominent feminists who are remembering their experience of the early women's liberation movement. In viewing these interviews through the lens of memory studies, I will argue that there are various ways oral narratives can dispute what has become sanctioned memory and provide alternatives to postmaternal thinking. The epigraph from Gail Jones's *Dreams of Speaking* is apposite here. Jones explores the inner dimensions of modernity in her novel, showing how the unmodern persists often at the very points when its demise appears immanent. Similarly, in interviews which speak directly of the advancements of feminist modernity, can the "language and love of that old mother culture,"[5] to return to Arlie Hochschild's resonant words, still be heard?

MILLENNIUM NARRATIVES

My analysis will be based on a selection of oral history interviews with well-known feminists who were active in the women's liberation movement and went on to achieve considerable success in political and executive arenas in Australia. While these interviews are held at the National Library of Australia, my focus will be on memories which do not rely on any national context for their meaning or wider significance. This is not to claim that these interviews are necessarily representative, but they do shed light on the intersection of public and private memory and different ways feminist history can be understood. Also, it should be noted that activist identities were often thoroughly globalized during this early period of the women's movement. These interviews reveal that women active in this emerging movement were reading the same kinds of authors—notably Shulamith Firestone, Kate Millett, Germaine Greer, and Betty Friedan—and discussing similar ideas as their counterparts in America, Britain, and Europe. Distinctively, however, Australian feminists played a unique role in state and federal bureaucracies in the 1970s and 1980s. It is prudent to remember it was in Australia that the term *femocrat* was developed both as a sign of the new power acquired by feminists in the bureaucracy and as a critical term used by other members of the women's movement to indicate the widening gap between activists and women in formal government positions. Femocrats centered on developing imaginative public policy to promote government-funded services for women. Unlike their counterparts in other countries, such as the U.S. and the UK, however, these women also had a direct line to prime ministers and state premiers.[6] Similarly, feminist academics in Australia had considerable influence in policy debates both nationally and internationally at this time. Consequently, these interviews provide rich and important memory texts.

The interviews relevant here all share certain characteristics. Once again, to return to Lynne Segal's words, they are ways of understanding "life backwards"[7] and include prominent feminists remembering the women's liberation movement.[8] The interviews also share a certain generational perspective. With few exceptions, the interviews are with women who discovered the women's movement at similar ages or life stages in the 1970s. Significantly, most interviews were conducted at the turn of the twentieth century. As narratives recorded at the millennium, they mirror the widespread view at the time that something had passed and was lost, never to be retrieved again. The interviews reflect the considerable historical and personal changes wrought from the early days of an emerging neoliberalism at the end of the 1970s to the dominance of neoliberal economic and cultural arrangements in the 1990s. Moreover, they coincide with and reproduce a growing cultural interest in memory at the time, a "memory wave" that was reflected in films, novels, popular discourse, and the rise of the memoir. Accordingly, a compelling way of viewing these oral history interviews is to see them as end-of-millennium narratives conducted during a personal testimony epidemic.

As influential historian Alistair Thomson reminds us, oral history (like memory) is shaped by particular social and intellectual forces.[9] As well as reflecting a generalized interest in life narratives and memory research,[10] the interactive approach to interviewing reflected in this collection also dramatizes later feminist critiques of positivist social science in the 1980s and the celebration of subjectivity as an important tool of analysis, rather than as a shortcoming of research.[11] Many of the *interviewers* also shared the experience of participation in the women's movement since its inception and in some cases are friends with the interview subjects. As examples of feminist rejection of the separation between researcher and researched, these interviews are dynamic and interactive. They follow informal conversational idioms with interjections, qualifications, and even at times disputes over respective memories of particular dates. Consequently, the kind of oral testimony under scrutiny provides pointed insight into the multifaceted relationship between personal and public memory.

MOSAICS OF MEMORY

The poetic and political force of oral narratives often resides in what Daniel James calls their "messiness," their paradoxical and contradictory nature.[12] Certainly some interview subjects attempt to shape reminiscences about their lives into neat, coherent, and somehow instructive accounts, such as what they may have learned from their experiences or how present circumstances appear to have logically emerged from their past. This process has been theorized by oral historians as the seeking of composure[13] or as the need to construct a "safe and necessary personal coherence out of risky, unresolved or painful pieces of past and present lives."[14] The concept of composure has a dual meaning. Following Graham Dawson, it refers to both the process of composing a life story and to the narrator striving to be composed, calm, and coherent.[15] A struggle for personal coherence is clearly evident in some of the recorded interviews with feminists in this collection. Close listening often reveals that such attempts are never entirely successful. Moreover, the interactive nature of the interviews to be discussed in what follows, the friendships and familiarity between the interviewers and interviewees, the breaks and interruptions, the interjections and shared involvement in memory production means there is ample space for contradictions, paradoxes, and discontinuities. This accords with Penny Summerfield's observation that composure is always provisional in life narratives and that feminist oral history practice may be more conducive to producing and revealing discomposure.[16]

In this respect, the strength of such oral testimonies can be their failure to entirely control the process of remembrance. This contrasts with the more stable versions of feminist history in academic texts and in public discourse. Interviews such as these refuse singular readings of key historical events. The tally sheet logic often underpinning popular discussions of the legacy of second-wave feminism (quantifying its successes and failures) is never wholly reproduced. A memory can invoke manifold responses, some of which are outside the dominant cultural scripts. This is particularly the case with Suzanne Bellamy's interview where she poetically proclaims, "The women's movement is my country."[17] Bellamy, artist, radical feminist, scholar, and writer, uses the metaphor of the mosaic in her oral history interview to describe her memories of the feminist movement: "This was never a period of unity. This was not a period in which everyone sat down and all agreed. It was a period of creative struggle out of the fantastic. It's like the palette was endless. The palette was, you know, it was a mosaic. . . . You can't set it up. But it was an explosive, creative struggle period."[18] At other points in this interview she remembers women's liberation as "an egg-laying extravaganza" and "one of those epoch-breaking periods that can only be sustained briefly, but within which everything is born." Her recollections depict the explosive spontaneity of the time as both "really precious" and as having "wounded everyone in various ways." Refusing the role of the auditor, retrospectively calculating the achievements or shortcomings of feminism, Bellamy instead embraces the disconnects of the day and resists the temptation to seek the composure or safety that some interpreters of oral history see as characteristic of personal testimony. This gives her particular interview an almost metanarrative quality where memories are recalled and theorized at the same time.

There's a sense if you're only going to look at a person's life as, like messy, that you'll say that they are sometimes connected with themselves and then they're sometimes disconnected with themselves. . . . But in an historical sense, that's often a useful creative tool for looking at movements of change, that they draw to them—first of all they draw to them a really disparate group. I mean, you know . . . that we drew to us the best and the worse, worse in inverted commas and best, because I think that we were the cream of our generation and also some of the most loopy.[19]

An example of the interactive nature of the interviews in this archive and the often reflective and irreverent approach to memory is in the following exchange. Bellamy is discussing, with the interviewer Biff Ward (a key interviewer in this collection), the relationship between the verbal and the visual in the women's movement, in poster art and in the layout of the first Australian women's liberation newspaper, *Mejane*.[20]

BW: My memory of it, just as you speak, is that it always had in terms of layout a kind of space—and it wasn't that there was a shortage of material, of blank spaces, but it wasn't as dense visually as everything else was at that time. It was almost as though there was room to breathe.

SB: That's good. That's good that that's your memory. I dare say I think that probably isn't true, but that's a wonderful memory, because the breadth was in there, in the idea—wasn't it? That's why you've got that memory possibly.[21]

If there is a particular template of remembrance informing how feminism is recalled, Suzanne Bellamy refuses to follow it. More than any other in these interviews, Bellamy rejects official versions of the women's movement as a story just about nation building or the integration of women into a nationalist narrative. Her reference points are not legislative changes or policy battles but the relationship between feminist anarchist guerrilla activism and art movements such as dada and surrealism. She refers to a secret history of feminism that has not yet been documented about such direct actions and the difficulty in finding an intellectual language creative enough to capture the underground narratives of the movement.

The concept of "enforced forgetting" employed by philosopher Jean Curthoys in *Feminist Amnesia: The Wake of Women's Liberation* is worth noting here. In this impressive and it would seem, much neglected study,[22] Curthoys examines the way certain prohibitions against identification with the early women's movement have emerged. "What is at issue may not be a straightforward forgetting of ideas which are, after all, now a quarter of a century old. This suggestion is reinforced when we realise that what we have is not only a forgotten history and a false history, but also, in some ways, an enforced false history. I mean by this that there is an effective prohibition in feminist intellectual circles of any positive identification with the early movement."[23] She points to simple, clear ideas being forced underground in the service of later manifestations of a power-oriented feminism. Her specific focus is a widespread amnesia about the centrality of liberation theory to the women's liberation movement. Her discussion of liberation theory goes back to Socratic and Christian worldviews. Essentially, she defines it as a moral position providing the key psychological power by abandoning the notion that "some people are more 'important' than others."[24] Jean Curthoys argues that the women's movement brought to life ideas that challenged ordinary and pervasive assumptions about human superiority and inferiority. She makes a range of compelling observations about what she sees as the forgetting of these ideas, claiming that there is almost a compulsory dissociation with the positive aspects of women's liberation. By "positive" here she means the broad-based, radically emancipatory ideas of the early women's liberation movement. In her view, feminism has subsequently been rewritten as a set of basically orthodox ideas.[25] One lasting effect is to make the enthusiasm, energy, and excitement (and unorthodox nature) of the early women's movement appear mysterious, odd, and difficult to explain.

Oral narratives can go a certain way to challenging this rewriting by documenting the creative and less orthodox elements of the women's liberation movement. Take for example the interview with Jill Julius Matthews, feminist historian and author of *Good and Mad Women: The Historical Construction of Femininity in Twentieth-Century Australia*.[26] Once again, like Suzanne Bellamy's interview, this testimony reflects the disorderly conduct associated with women's liberation and not its later, more docile version. Memories of music and cultural protest, the different expressions of women's culture in the Australian cities of Adelaide and Melbourne, and the details of the first women's liberation posters are richly drawn in this interview. Matthews recalls the times not as "the unfolding of activism into a career path,"[27] but rather as a period when, Matthews proudly declares: "We were absolutely rabid."[28] The extent to which feminist cultural radicalism has been eclipsed or, to use terms from memory theory, actively forgotten is a topic for another time. I concur with Margaret Henderson's persuasive observation, in her illuminating essay "The Tidiest Revolution," that the autobiographies and histories of Australian feminism, in particular those that emerged in the mid to late 1990s, tend toward a persistent othering of radical politics.[29]

Henderson highlights the way memoirs of prominent feminists, such as former Australian federal cabinet minister Susan Ryan's *Catching the Waves*, corporate leader Wendy McCarthy's *Don't Fence Me In,* or journalist and former editor of *Ms.* Anne Summers's *Ducks on the Pond*, flatten out experiences and domesticate the women's movement. She quotes a review by celebrated novelist Drusilla Modjeska, who observed that in these memoirs it is possible to get a good sense of what these women have done but "not much of who they are."[30] Henderson carefully details the way (ironically) a specifically masculine kind of subjectivity is fashioned from the "limited engagement with the intersection of fantasy, desire, the irrational and the emotional in the subject of women's movement politics."[31] Perhaps this is where certain national characteristics come into play. The formal public success of Australian feminists and their acceptance into the mainstream may colonize or distort earlier memories. This biographical writing may unwittingly contribute to the idea that everything was to be subsumed in the service of career and labor market participation. According to Henderson, the women's movement becomes domesticated and regulated in these textual accounts:

> Such a version is in accord with the general outline of a feminist past offered by the dominant culture, and even by certain feminists. In effect, the three autobiographies appear to be strangely out of time and place in relation to feminist debates of the last couple of decades, whether about cultural politics, theories of subjectivity, or speaking position. This is ironic, given that the texts are concerned to present accounts of radical social change, and that they (justifiably) evince a great desire to be part of history.[32]

It is worth briefly noting that this toned-down version of feminist activism is not as evident in biographies and histories coming out of the United States. Nor is there such a dearth of studies reexamining the countercultural and radical dimensions of the early women's movement.[33] A case in point is Alice Echols's *Daring to Be Bad: Radical Feminism in America, 1967–1975* and her *Shaky Ground: The Sixties and Its Aftershocks*. In the latter she opens with the slogan "Eat Shit: Ten Million Flies Can't be Wrong!"[34] By contrast, in Australian feminist autobiographies the subject is not "wild girls," according to Henderson, but "big girls."[35] She argues that feminist subjects emerge as special, usually by virtue of career achievements. The autobiographical self is presented as not too different, too strange, or too radical.[36] Henderson also asks the important question, how might a feminist activist's life be narrated in a feminist mode?[37] One answer might be to look toward oral reminiscence.

The impulse to definitively capture and pin down the legacy of diverse and disruptive forms of protest seems perhaps more difficult to resist in written records of social movements. It is an impulse that is rejected in Bellamy's use of the metaphor of the women's movement as an endless mosaic. Similarly, Todd Gitlin, former Students for a Democratic Society activist, author, and commentator, uses the idea of a "sand painting" to indicate that the outcomes and meanings of social movements are always provisional and shifting in historical time.[38] Interpretive strategies from memory studies and oral history provide a useful framework for keeping this provisionality firmly in view.

RESISTING THE CULTURAL SCRIPT

Oral historians grapple with questions about the relationship between individual and collective memory and whether personal recollection always follows a cultural script.[39] The oral narratives of Bellamy and Matthews, and many others in the National Library of Australia collection, illustrate that there is "space for the consciously reflective individual," to use Anna Green's phrase, and that oral reminiscence is *not* always determined by a preexisting cultural script.[40] Green raises questions about cultural theorizations of memory that devalue or reject notions of individual memory. She argues that the cultural and linguistic turn in memory theory has risked a form of cultural determinism where personal reflection is always subsumed under the rubric of a collective, social memory.[41] Green convincingly contests the automatic conflation of individual and collective memory. In reference to the wider field of cultural history, Wulf Kansteiner also suggests a growing unease with the failure of memory studies to sufficiently conceptualize individual autobiographical memory as distinct from collective memory.[42]

While cultural scripts about feminist modernity, and women as instrumental in making the nation truly "modern" do surface in these interviews, individual reminiscence can depart from these dominant narratives. The link between market participation and women's emancipation, so central to public cultural memory of second-wave feminism, is not always reproduced in memories of private experience. Certain interviews make this point entirely unprompted. Take for instance the

2001 interview with Meredith Burgmann, writer and activist and member of the New South Wales Legislative Council from 1991–2007. Burgmann discusses how in the early 1970s she could easily have stayed in the United States, where she was teaching gridiron at the time, if she hadn't had to return to Australia for a legal appeal after being arrested protesting the 1971 South African Springboks's rugby tour:

> Don't forget in those days I didn't have any ambition because ambition was wrong, and I still don't really. It has never occurred to me that I've got to get in there and work hard and make my way up the ladder, that's just totally foreign to, I mean it was a bit foreign to the way I was . . . and that was compounded by the 1960s view that any form of ambition was anti-revolutionary, and I still feel that way, I find very ambitious people quite blood chilling. I don't know quite how to deal with them. I have never really known what I wanted to do. I mean, I've ended up in a very strange job which no-one actually knows what you do in it, and it quite suits me, but that's all totally by accident.[43]

It would be mistaken to dismiss such observations as misrepresentations, where public success is portrayed as somehow accidental, thereby further underscoring the achievements of the narrator. Nor is this an example of what Jean Curthoys might call an enforced forgetting of personal motivation. More recent evidence of Burgmann's rejection of careerism is that she resigned as president of the New South Wales Parliament's Legislative Council (perhaps the U.S. equivalent might be the speaker of the California or New York Legislative Assembly) to pursue a different form of political activism as a member of Sydney's City Council. The point here is that oral testimonies, such as Burgmann's and others in this collection, provide a more multifaceted picture of personal ambition, public life, and activist identity. In this respect, viewing life backward can be a form of active remembering, with its own politics of resisting contemporary depictions of feminism's legacy. Burgmann's reminiscences about the alien nature of any form of ambition represent both a genuine discomfort about careerism (then and now) and a personal challenge to sanctioned collective memory.

The close listening theorized by Rhonda Williams is a useful tool to detect memories that in other contexts may have been discarded. Listening to oral accounts, where the emotional intensity of feminist recollection is so palpable, a self-critical history of the women's liberation movement emerges, resisting fixed and monolithic categories. As all oral historians would know, the aural experience of listening to the interview is crucial to unearthing this plurality of meanings. A written transcript does not provide access to the wild laughter provoked by particular memories or the performative aspects of an interview. Listening to the interviewees struggle with the contradictory emotions produced by the process of recall, and their efforts to compose a coherent narrative of disparate fragments, provides a vivid glimpse into the personal and public stakes of feminist involvement. A case in point is a recent interview with Susan Magarey, founding editor of *Australian Feminist Studies* and founding director of the Research Centre for Women's Studies at the University of Adelaide. Magarey is an academic and prize-winning author of biographies of Australian women. The interviewer, Sara Dowse, is one of the key interviewers in this collection. Dowse is also a prize-winning author and women's rights activist and, notably, for this discussion, was the inaugural head of the Women's Affairs Section of the Department of Prime Minister and Cabinet (now the Office of the Status of Women) in the Whitlam Labor government in 1974. Magarey remembers a point in her own life when she "began to have some sense of actually having a *career* rather than a *job*."[44] Dowse passionately intervenes at this point in the interview. She recounts her own experience of being interviewed by a PhD student about the women's movement. She comments: "She interviewed me, and one of the things I was very clear about was that, for that women's lib period, that was so life changing for us, I, I can't remember many of us thinking in terms of career."[45] Significantly, Sara Dowse resigned from public office as head of the Women's Affairs section of the federal government in 1977 in order to pursue her writing.

Aside from being one of the distinguished oral history interviewers for the National Library, Sara Dowse is also interviewed twice in this collection. Questions about her resignation arise in these interviews, but also surface in others where Dowse is in the role of interviewer. However, the vehemence with which she rejects the notion of being motivated by career ambition is striking in this more recent interview with Susan Magarey. She is more adamant in 2008 about her lack of career ambition than when interviewed nearly a decade earlier about her life. This highlights another way in which oral narratives are in dialogue with and shaped by contemporary representations of the past. After making the point that her own pursuit of writing had nothing to do with wealth or career advancement, Dowse continues, seeking confirmation from Magarey (the interviewee).

SD: I mean in fact, we were very critical of any kind of careerism.

SM: Yes.

SD: You know, this was, this was individual advancement and we weren't interested in that! (This is followed by a comment about her writing also not being about individual advancement.)

SD: I mean, there we were. We then suddenly found ourselves in these positions. I in the bureaucracy—you in the university!

SM: And doing it.

SD: Where, I mean, yes, we had a different approach then. It was more that, we would, you know, change the world by changing that institution. And even so, in a way, I find it particularly hurtful the, the accusations that we get from a lot of contemporary women, that we were all just interested in careers.

SM: Oh, that's bullshit.

SD: And I mean it was just so untrue.

SM: Yeah, it's absolute bullshit.

SD: And, and, that we were willing to forsake everything else for our advancement! Well I never was like that. Never! I found it gratifying, yes, that I had achieved something in this world. Yes of course, but

I never had that [careerism]. And I don't think any of us had that
singleness of purpose.[46]

This is an example of the aural being crucial to understanding this interaction. A transcript fails to capture the dialogic and social context of the
oral history interview where shared perceptions are produced and disputed through conscious reflection on the process of self-representation.

The energy and emotional charge of the period can also be heard
in the recorded interviews. Feminist history has long been predicated
on an interest in the emotional lives of women. Yet, as Henderson has
argued, histories and memoirs of the women's movement can also be
strangely devoid of affect. This is all the more puzzling given the genu-
inely passionate commitment to the idea of the personal as political at
the time. The reflections of Lynne Segal, in her *Making Trouble: Life and
Politics,* are a case in point. It is a book opening with the provocation
"This is not a memoir."[47] Segal rejects popular and scholarly assess-
ments of second-wave feminism as a form of historical revisionism and
tries to do something different in recalling her own political journey.
She offers a "portrait of a political moment, placing oneself within it,
however cautiously, knowing the limits of retrospection."[48] Her detailed
reminiscences make compelling reading partly because her experiences
are so unconventional, on the one hand, and so typical of the day, on
the other.

Unlike the oral narratives discussed here, Segal chooses to recall
the details of campaigns and struggles more than the feelings and emotions they inflamed. Aside from the extracts from other people's letters
and memoirs, *Making Trouble* is notable for and perhaps constrained
by its relatively impersonal voice. As Henderson has shown, this is also
a feature of other feminist memoirs. Segal attempts to distinguish herself from such writing by repeating that her book is not meant to be a
confessional narrative. Yet, with the exception of a brief section in her
chapter on aging, this silence around her interior life works to undermine the gendered and embodied and, in short, the feminist nature of

the narrative. The struggle for composure or personal equanimity is at the expense of registering the emotional texture of the experiences that are remembered.

By contrast, the "affective turn" in cultural and critical theory is evident in recent attempts to theorize the way emotion works to inform and inspire action.[49] These oral histories of the women's movement are stories of passionate attachments: to political ideals, to activist identities, to utopian senses of feminist community, to other women, and to particular forms of cultural expression. They are also stories of loss, of political and personal rivalries, of anxieties, angers, and disappointments. If these affective dimensions of the women's movement are culturally forgotten and are absent from the public discourse, then there is little wonder that popular representations of a career-obsessed feminism take hold.

BURIED MATERNALISM

Attention to the affective dimensions of feminist reminiscence can work to challenge the dominance of what has become sanctioned feminist cultural memory. The relatively impersonal voice of many of the textual representations, as discussed in the previous section of this chapter, may contribute to postmaternal thinking. This is particularly true of the naturalized opposition between feminism and motherhood. Twenty-first-century memories of feminism as antichild, or as promising that women could "have it all," or as being responsible for the work-obsessed career woman, are widely circulated in the public domain. Anxieties about the historical accuracy of these representations often surface in the opinion pages of newspapers, online discussion, and in scholarly articles and debates. In oral recollections it is striking to note how frequently memories do not conform to postmaternal perspectives and do not reproduce the "women as nation builders" cultural script. Some of the interviews under scrutiny directly record the difficult efforts by early second-wave feminists to tackle issues affecting the lives of mothers and young children. These memories are not recounted in abstract, gender-neutral policy language. Instead, campaigns around refuges (women's shelters), violence against women, rape crisis centers, or child care are rendered as emotionally fraught, disturbing, and often contradictory experiences. A history of affect is recorded as well as a narrative of key events. In my view, the oral record here unearths a maternalist ethos that has been forgotten or hidden in many contemporary renderings of feminism's complex legacy.

While Sara Ruddick reminds us of the significance of maternal thinking to feminist politics and theory,[50] others define the women's liberation movement by its negative stance toward the maternalism of the so-called first wave. In *Australian Feminism: A Companion,* Marilyn Lake divides the Australian women's movement into five overlapping phases. She traces the way a maternalist orientation was discarded in the struggle for equal opportunity (the 1940s to the 1960s) and replaced by the language of citizenship and then the language of revolution in the 1970s.[51] Maternalism, as I have already indicated, is an ambiguous and often problematic political configuration. Lake clearly documents this complexity in a fine historical study, *Getting Equal: The History of Australian Feminism.*[52] Ruddick similarly describes maternal politics as always "partial, imperfect and limited by context."[53] Yet a form of maternalism does resurface in oral history recollections of an activism that had, as one of its central aims, to transform the concerns of mothers and children from a private responsibility into public policy.[54] The nurturing impulses of this kind of activism seem to have been overshadowed or buried in the collective memory of the women's movement. It is as though there has been a cultural forgetting of the nurturing feminist, so much so that even putting the two terms together feels distinctly uncomfortable. However, cross-generational examples from the oral history record illustrate that the language of love and protection—seen to be a characteristic of a phase of feminism—is not neutralized by the emergence of other more self-consciously political calls for equality, citizenship, or revolution.

Observe, for example, Ann Turner's interview with Phyllis Johnson in 1995. I have included this interview because it illustrates a feminist activism that spans the whole of the twentieth century. Johnson, who describes herself as a "lifelong campaigner for women's equality," was born in 1917 and went on her first International Women's Day March in 1936. In her oral history interview, Johnson describes what she calls the "tender loving care" that was given to the women and children who came to the Betsy Women's Refuge in Bankstown in 1975.[55] While she discusses the rallies and protests outside Parliament that were organized at the time and the slogan "no silence against domestic violence," Johnson's language is expressly maternal. She describes how she and other feminists would cook meals for the women and children when they first arrived at the refuge. Her words and her emphatic tone reveal a different picture to that of militant feminist ideologues discussing patriarchal power relations and women's collectivities with the victims of domestic violence, as depicted in some written histories of the period.[56] Johnson looks back on this time and, rather, remembers the nurturing: "Oh the love, the love that we gave the children—the cuddles and the cosseting."[57]

Not surprisingly, the term *cosseting* does not recur in the other interviews or in written accounts of later feminist activism. However, nurturing impulses do resurface in these oral narratives. For instance, Biff Ward recalls how ill-equipped many feminists were when working in the first refuges, unprepared for the experiences that would confront them. She discusses the grief she and others felt about the children of women who came seeking protection from violence:

Another memory I have is of a meeting, a staff meeting, where we decided, we had a major topic for this weekly meeting and we were going to finally really talk about the children. . . . Virtually everybody in the room had enormous distress around these children and could hardly bear to look at them, and tried to kind of look over their heads all the time and to avoid . . . I mean, everyone had different things, but all of them were just saying "my grief in looking at these children is too great and I can't bear it."[58]

Julia Ryan, feminist, educator, and a founding member of the National Foundation of Australian Women, speaks in her oral history interview about the emotional intensity of refuge work: "Although I was not actually directly involved in any terrible incidents with guns or violence, just the whole feeling of tension all the time, and the misery and the hardness of it, I found it very, very demoralising."[59] She remembers how one of her roles was to provide statistics at the end of each month, calculating the number of women and children who had come to the refuge in search of a safe environment. She would frequently be unwell during this time and only later realized the connection between her empathy for the women and children and her physical illness. Both interviews, in recording the affective dimensions of feminist activism, open a space where postmaternal thinking can be challenged.

This is not to downplay tensions around the maternal, nor to overlook the divisions around motherhood, reproduction, and care in what American critical theorist Seyla Benhabib calls the "paradigm wars of feminist theory."[60] Much has been written on these issues.[61] My purpose is not to reproduce these debates. Rather, by paying close attention to oral sources, my aim is to suggest a counternarrative to the dominant historical account. Anna Green calls on us to more closely heed the ways individuals negotiate competing belief systems or find spaces between dominant discourses.[62] Unearthing a maternalist ethos in these memories of early feminist activism is an attempt to follow this directive and locate one such space between discourses.

The profound skepticism toward career evident in these retrospective accounts of the period simply is not a feature of popular depictions of the historical legacy of mid-twentieth-century feminism. Instead, contemporary ideas about the work/family divide or the work/life balance seem to be projected back in time to give shape and meaning to dominant cultural memories. Segal finds the current figure of the career-obsessed feminist difficult to recognize. She writes: "Today's career woman resides in a world apart from those alternative dreams of mutuality back then, when troubling dilemmas around self-reliance and personal authenticity meshed with the desire to create a better world in ways that were decidedly 'anti-careerist.'"[63] Similarly, as I have argued, the seemingly naturalized alliance between feminism and career is problematized in these oral narratives. The interviews depart from culturally prevailing assumptions about work-centered feminism. Unexpectedly irreverent attitudes toward paid work are expressed. This is a far cry from the image of the movement's main achievement as paving a solid career path for women. Stories of the difficulty in finding employment and of stumbling by chance upon suitable jobs are frequently told.

On a related point, the depiction of children as a primary impediment to career promotion seems also to be a later construction, if these interviews are in any way representative. It would appear that once careerism is taken out of the picture, a different portrait emerges. Memories of motherhood and children and their impact on feminist subjectivity take on a less conflicted complexion. Dowse, for example, remembers her children as being a distinct advantage in the policy arena when she was the inaugural head of the Women's Affairs Section of the Australian Department of Prime Minister and Cabinet.

There were two things that helped me—apart from my feminism and being, if you like, an expert because nobody else in the department had a clue. First, I had no ambitions in this area at all. I was truly a disinterested public servant. I didn't envisage spending the rest of my life as a bureaucrat. I was surprised to discover what a good bureaucrat I could be, but I had no ambitions there. The second thing was having kids. . . . You know, if you have to go home and cook the dinner, you can't take yourself all that seriously. It's a grounding . . . You can be in an absolutely tremendous combat, a subtle but nonetheless tremendous combat in an interdepartmental committee, and go home and have to look for the frozen peas! I knew that there was nobody else in the department that had that experience. If they had to go home to dinner, their wives would just present it to them. Although it made it easier in some ways, it isolated them terribly and did bad things to their egos. So, you know, I think that those things did see me through what proved to be a very, very hectic, dynamic time.[64]

Such observations refuse the current binary conception of an unbridgeable divide between work and family or what Talbot calls the "radical incommensurability of home and work."[65] Is it possible that feminist entanglements with individualist, neoliberal definitions of work (as the source of all meaning) are a more recent historical phenomenon than is currently thought?

It is interesting to briefly compare the memories recalled by Dowse with the writings about maternal subjectivity discussed in the preceding chapter: the confessional narratives of Naomi Wolf in *Misconceptions*, Rachel Cusk in *A Life's Work,* or Rebecca Walker in *Baby Love*. Aside from the generational differences here, the idea of pregnancy and motherhood as a detailed, disciplinary regime of endless self-surveillance seems to be a relatively new configuration.[66] This observation will be more fully developed in the next chapter in a critique of the collection *The Maternal Is Political* and of various online expressions of the new mothers' movement. To return to the interviews, however, Dowse compellingly links children with creativity rather than as a threat to the clearly individuated self. Her decision to have another child, in difficult circumstances and against the advice of many of her friends in the women's movement, is depicted as integral to her sense of herself as a feminist.

I was always good at taking into account, but not listening to everybody around me, not saying I must do something because other people think so, but really sitting down and working out what was important for me. I hadn't been thinking of another child, and my life could have been easier, I suppose, but it was what I had to have. It was who I was.

So that to me is feminism. To be able to really feel confident in that skin. If there's any achievement, that's it. To realize, oh, yes, I'm a writer and what this has meant. Of course, I would have thought as I did in 1970. Of course I wouldn't have gone along with the group. Of course, I'd be a maverick. Whereas once that worried me, or I was made to feel that it was worrisome, I'm proud of it now. And I look at this wonderful eighteen-year-old boy and I think, you know, I did that. But more than what I gave to him is what he gave to me at a time when all the joy had been taken out of life. He gave that back to me.[67]

A complicated feminist subjectivity is expressed here. On the one hand, there is a sense of individualism not threatened by connectedness but rather strengthened by children and the maternal and, on the other, a self-identified feminism expressed as standing apart from the group. This mix of tensions and contradictions underscores the problems with stable definitions of feminism and calls for different modes of inquiry into women's activism and women's movements.

As signaled at the opening of this book, the dominance of neoliberalism in the past few decades is fused with the way maternalism has been forgotten or written out of the cultural script by those opposing and those supporting feminist perspectives. In the U.S. the absence of a well-developed welfare state, with adequately funded child care, health, and social policies, has meant that second-wave feminists achieved fewer major changes to government social programs before the surge of right-wing policy agendas of the 1980s and 1990s. By contrast, Australian feminists were more successful in transforming social policy regimes to the benefit of women and children. While maternalist directions in policy making at this time may be repudiated or ignored in subsequent retrospective written accounts, the oral record tells a different story. It is therefore revealing that, despite the championing of diverse policies to tackle gender inequality at a social level, the dominant, contemporary public image of feminists during this period is one of career-obsessed free-market individuals. Just as Robinson Crusoe became emblematic of the "economical rational" individual of early capitalism, second-wave feminism has somehow become synonymous with the neoliberalism of late capitalism. Paradoxically, the rich and varied history of feminism has been reduced to an agenda that elevated work-centered values above all else, including communal and interpersonal perspectives based on care, nurturance, and mutuality.

I have attempted to suggest that the emotional dimensions of oral narratives can provide a significant alternative, affective history of the women's movement. In this counterhistory, diverse motivations and desires are recorded and multifaceted, mosaic-like pictures of second-wave feminism emerge. Uncovering a buried maternalism is an effort to resist dominant representational frameworks about worked-centered feminism and move toward more open-ended and self-questioning dialogues about the maternal.

Familiar, public renderings of feminism's history often depict the women's movement as an inexorable march toward modernity. If women were to become modern, emancipated subjects, certain things would have to be left behind. The so-called ancient maternal ties were seen to be the first to go. While this celebratory narrative of feminist modernity, the women-as–nation-builders cultural script, may capture significant dimensions of the women's movement, it reinforces what I have called postmaternal thinking: a widespread cultural anxiety around nurture and care. Moreover, this script plays a crucial role in what Jean Curthoys describes as the rewriting of feminism as a set of basically orthodox ideas.[68] If, alongside maternalism, the more heterodox, creative, and profane elements of women's liberation have long been forgotten, it is no wonder that we are left with a hollowed out and publicly sanctioned version of the past. As I have argued, this version naturalizes an opposition between feminism and maternal forms of subjectivity and strengthens neoliberal policy agendas. Remembering some of the nurturing impulses underpinning early second-wave activism creates a space for less conventional imaginings and may point to alternative conceptions of a new maternalist feminist politics for the future.

4

Maternalism Reconfigured?

> I value nurturing and caring because it is good, not because
> it constitutes women's "difference."
>
> CAROL J. ADAMS, "Caring about Suffering"

espite the widespread repudiation of maternalism in social policy, public discourse, and in sanctioned memories of second-wave feminism, it would appear that resistance to postmaternal thinking is gaining momentum. Witness the debates about whether there is a new mothers' movement sweeping the United States and the proliferation of maternal online advocacy groups. Other cultural manifestations have emerged in the form of conferences on motherhood in the twenty-first century, Mama Festivals, a Museum of Motherhood, rock concerts celebrating motherhood, and mamazines. A range of products have been launched announcing whether you are an Outlaw Mom, a Hot Mama, or a Green Mom.[1] Mothers are purportedly "rising" through blogging, twittering, publishing, singing, and speaking out in new and energetic ways that draw consciously on a repertoire of themes about maternal identity. It would be easy, perhaps, to conclude that Mom has been well and truly branded. On the other hand, it is possible also to concur with a *New York Times* article in 2007 declaring, "Mom's Mad. And She's Organized."[2] In discussing the manifesto of the group Moms Rising, and other loose coalitions of advocacy groups around motherhood, the *New York*

Times piece documents a burgeoning movement organizing around family and economic issues. The extent to which this whirl of online activity around motherhood actually reflects a reconfigured maternalism will be one focus of this chapter. The chapter will also address other manifestations of maternal activism and maternalist impulses in popular culture. It is important to examine different forms of resistance to a privatized motherhood. Also, in discussing new attempts to extend maternal forms of subjectivity from the private to the public domain, it is necessary to reflect on the paradoxical and conflicted relationship between feminism and maternalism.

The idea of mothering as a paradigm of care is usually at the heart of maternalist movements. To return to the definition of maternalism discussed in preceding chapters, the term refers to "ideologies and discourses that exalted women's capacity to mother and applied to society as a whole, the values that they attached to that role: care, nurturance and morality."[3] Criticisms of maternalism cover a range of positions. This includes attacks on the gender traditionalism inherent in how motherhood is apparently defined by maternalists, feminist critiques of the normative ideals of a male breadwinner and female homemaker and the related charges of essentialism, where motherhood is universalized and not dependent on culture or context. However, studies of the gendered history of the welfare state seem to be divided on whether maternalist campaigns in the past aimed to transform the foundations of the social order or leave conventional ideologies of motherhood intact. In "The Selfless and the Helpless: Maternalist Origins of the U.S. Welfare State," Patrick Wilkinson provides a thoughtful analysis of the scholarship in this area from the 1990s. He highlights the unexpected historical arguments to emerge in these studies, including the work of Eileen Boris in *Home to Work: Motherhood and the Politics of Industrial Homework in the United States*, Linda Gordon's *Pitied But not Entitled: Single Mothers and the History of Welfare*, Gwendolyn Mink's *The Wages of Motherhood: Inequality in the Welfare State, 1917–1943*, and Theda Skocpol's *Protecting Soldiers and Mothers: The Political Origins of Social Policy in the United*

States. Wilkinson identifies a point at which these studies converge, namely, in "a shared recognition that the movement was defined and bounded by the very conditions that enabled its success."[4] The ideas and forces that animated and motivated maternalist campaigns in the first part of the twentieth century in America also set limits on what could be achieved. In short, according to the abovementioned scholars, gender-based arguments for state expansion in the name of protecting women and children were based on conventional ideals of motherhood, which constrained the progressive force of their own policy initiatives.

Wilkinson advances this argument by reference to Gwendolyn Mink's discussion of the mothers' pensions that were introduced across many U.S. states between 1920 and 1930. These were direct payments to impoverished women authorized by state-level statutes and can be seen to be the forerunner to the Aid to Dependent Children Portion of the U.S. Social Security Act of 1935. At first sight, mothers' pensions promised "full political dignity and citizenship to poor women."[5] However, according to Wilkinson's reading of the evidence, the pensions had a contradictory effect. Middle-class white women linked poor women's pension entitlements to class-based and racialized ideas about motherhood. In this respect, the pensions, which in the main were for immigrant and poor Afro-American women, came with a price, the adoption of a "uniform cultural standard of motherhood and family life" imposed on others by maternalist campaigners.[6]

Such glimpses into the history of American maternalism can provide a useful framework for an investigation of the contemporary *neomaternalism* of mothers' movements in the twenty-first century. Skocpol's detailed observations about maternalist campaigns at the turn of last century are a case in point. She identifies a broad array of protective labor regulations and social benefits enacted from 1900 to 1920 "to help adult American women as mothers or as potential mothers."[7] As Wilkinson notes, Skocpol argues that there was a particularly apt fit between the organizational structures of local women's clubs and federations, their maternalist claims, and the political institutions and culture of the time.

Able to rely on their own federated network of local, state-level, and national organizations, they could bypass the divisive and conservative process of party mobilization, while at the same time coordinating campaigns that targeted all levels of the decentralized government simultaneously. And as women advocating women-oriented reforms in a political system already premised on the notion of "separate spheres," they operated from a position of moral authority that male judges, administrators, and legislators, who otherwise opposed welfare measures, had been socially conditioned to cede them.[8]

These observations are relevant to the discussion to follow. When examining the emergence of mothers' movements in the current period, questions arise about the fit between their aims and claims and the postmaternal political and social culture described in the previous chapters. Are these new movements advocating "women-oriented" reforms? Does their emergence signal a reconfigured maternalism or simply a more general call for recognition of maternal experiences and identity? Do these movements, of mainly middle-class professional women, paradoxically reinforce neoliberal ideas of the self-sufficient individual at the same time that they celebrate motherhood? And what complex processes of memory and forgetting are at play in these attempts to promote new forms of maternal thinking?

HEARING MOTHERS THINKING

According to Sara Ruddick, whenever mothers meet together "at their jobs, in playgrounds, or over coffee," they can be "heard thinking."[9] It is possible to listen to this thinking in the numerous and diverse online mothers' networks that together constitute the so-called new mothers' movement. Before briefly venturing into the intricate web of some of these groups and organizations, it is worth reviewing once again Ruddick's original conception of maternal thinking. In her view, complex cognitive processes and intellectual capacities develop from the practice of mothering. These include a particular kind of moral attentiveness involving reasoning, judgment, criteria for determining failure or success, conceptions of truth, and the identification of specific virtues. However, Ruddick also says that, when mothers can be heard thinking, this does not "necessarily mean that they can be heard being good."[10] Refusing to sentimentalize motherhood, or reduce it to something instinctual or exclude men from maternal thought and practice, Ruddick develops an idea of mothering as a profoundly intellectual activity.[11]

The proliferation and sheer creativity of social online communities around mothering and online advocacy networks certainly demonstrate the forms of reasoning and cognitive capacities Ruddick identifies as maternal thinking. There are even Web sites that reference Ruddick's idea in their titles, such as *Mothers Who Think* or *Brain, Child: The Magazine for Thinking Mothers*.[12] It would be impossible to do justice to the range of groups here. Nor would it be feasible to represent the scope and emotional charge in the variety of debates that take place in an assortment of virtual sites. It almost seems as though each week new Web-based mothers' organizations emerge in the U.S., the UK, or Australia.[13] In the case of one British group, *Mumsnet*, the prime minister and politicians from all political persuasions were joining Web chats on the site and courting the group's wide membership in an effort to win the mother's vote in the May 2010 British elections.[14] Such groups attempt to formulate alternative policy around family and leave arrangements, to provide parenting advice, and, in the case of the UK, run regular election polls of its members. Other groups, to be discussed, have more wide-reaching global aims and perspectives.

Even a cursory survey of postings and discussion of some of these online groups uncovers comments that range from the personal to the deeply philosophical. If indeed this represents a new Internet-based mothers' movement, one thing is abundantly clear, the perspectives encompassed are far from homogeneous. According to Lori Kido Lopez in her article "The Radical Act of 'Mommy Blogging': Redefining Motherhood

Through the Blogosphere," the most popular blog sites dealing with motherhood can attract more than fifty thousand hits per day and collect hundreds of comments per entry.[15] However, in her own textual analysis of twenty-one blogs that mentioned the phrase "mommy blogging is a radical act," she found that "white, married, heterosexual women" dominated the conversation in this online community.[16] She also noted the fact that many postings came from the U.S. rather than other regions. Her investigation also challenged the stereotype that all "mommy bloggers are stay-at-home moms."[17] She found that the participants were from a mix of full-time and part-time working mothers, and others who worked from home. While this may be representative of the small section of the blogosphere analyzed by Lopez, such observations are reproduced in the collection of essays *Motherhood and Blogging: The Radical Act of the MommyBlog*.[18] Here blogs are viewed as challenging the distinction between private and public motherhood and as a practice with creative, social, and political elements.[19]

A snapshot of some of the groups in the new mothers' movement reveals some interesting characteristics. Starting with the most self-consciously global of these groups, *Mothers Acting Up,* the membership is different to that identified in Lopez's survey. This organization boasts groups in twenty-four different countries and members from over fifty U.S. states. *Mothers Acting Up* has a distinctive transnational reach and an overt mission to mobilize on behalf of the world's children. In many ways, the group promotes a maternalist ethos for action that would not be out of place in campaigns of the early part of the twentieth century. Accordingly, they invite mothers "to stretch [their] traditional mother roles to include publicly and passionately advocating for the world's children."[20] An impressive array of issues and campaigns are showcased on their Web site. These revolve around three central concerns: child security, sustainability (clean water and climate change), and global child poverty.[21] While the organization may promote a maternal vision of mothers mobilizing to nurture children everywhere, it is perhaps at this point that its similarity to earlier movements ends. Rather, *Mothers*

Acting Up shares more characteristics with contemporary global social movements and networks than with the maternalism of the past. For instance, it operates in a sphere which has very little to do with the nation-state, and its actions are both virtual (online activism) and concrete. While it calls on mothers to engage in collective action, it also urges members to record their individual, daily actions. According to social movement theorist Michel Wieviorka, this is one of the defining features of the new global movements. Individuals are encouraged to manage their own participation in their own way.[22] Another defining characteristic identified by Wieviorka and clearly exhibited by *Mothers Acting Up* is an attempt to develop new and expressive forms of cultural life through activism and protest. *Mothers Acting Up* sets out five principles that guide the group. The first of these is to "be exuberant," because activism, particularly that executed with "children at one's side," needs to be both sustainable and joyful.[23] This principle ensures that this movement avoids the piety often attributed to earlier maternalist campaigns, while keeping children as active participants and firmly in the groups' sights.

A brief examination of other groups in this new mothers' movement shows that they can be far less child focused. This perhaps reflects another aspect of the diversity of the movement under question. *Mothers & More*, for example, gives specific priority to the needs of mothers.[24] It presents itself as an international movement, yet it began as a national support group for women whose careers had been interrupted by having children. This focus is evident in its original guise as *F.E.M.A.L.E* (Formerly Employed Mothers at the Leading Edge). It is an organization with a twenty-year history and, in this respect, is much older than other online mothers' networks. Interestingly, its membership reflects a highly educated population. According to its own statistics, 86 percent have college degrees and 35 percent have a masters or PhD.[25] It is difficult to determine if this is representative of other groups in the mothers' movement. Given the online nature of much activism, and Lopez's findings, it may be fair to assume that a significant proportion of members are also from highly educated, professional backgrounds. While *Mothers & More* makes use of Internet-based campaigning strategies, the group is less recognizable as a global social movement in the terms just discussed. Despite its international mission, the map of the movement's various chapters remains that of the United States. In other ways it appears more like a lobbying group than *Mothers Acting Up* and tackles a range of issues around employment and individual rights.

Mothers & More illustrates some of the ambiguities in the relationship between these movements and maternalist perspectives. Judith Stadtman Tucker, founder and editor of the Web-based journal *Mothers Movement Online,* attempts to map the ideological roots of some of these groups. In "Motherhood and Its Discontents: The Political and Ideological Grounding of the Twenty-first-Century Mothers Movement," she identifies three frameworks used by mothers' movements to promote social reform: liberal feminism, maternalism, and feminist care theory.[26] She points to maternalist threads in the rhetoric of *Mothers & More* that combine with the liberal feminist language of individual rights. While I do not agree with all of Tucker's typologies, her discussion of this group is instructive. On the maternalist side, *Mothers & More* claims broad recognition for the social value of care. The group calls for the meaning and value of work to be redefined to include the work of unpaid caregiving. On the other hand, individual choice is championed, and the emphasis is on improving the lives of mothers through discrete reforms rather than through the extension of maternal values to the whole society.

Even a brief excursion into the activist Web sites of groups like *Mothers & More* can lead to some unsettling observations. This is not to detract from the vigor and critical potential of this emerging movement as a whole. Rather, it is to recognize an underlying tension between its maternalist impulses and a much more widespread cultural unease with any type of dependency, including the care and nurture required by children. For some Internet-based mothers' organizations this is a deliberate shift of focus away from children (or the relationship between mothers and children) to maternal forms of self-expression.[27] The recognition and communication of motherhood as a challenging new identity becomes of paramount importance. Certainly this constitutes a dynamic resistance to a privatized view of motherhood, where the labor, care, and love are hidden from public view. Indeed, visibility is a key signifier in the discourse promoting maternal expression on these sites. In many ways these communities of mothers challenge the public/private dichotomy and play a significant role in creating a new, virtual, interactive public sphere. However, these sites do not always represent a resistance to dominant cultural understandings of family, work, and the values of the market. There is a tension, palpable at times, between an idealized self-sufficient, unencumbered individualism, on the one hand, and notions of selfless motherhood, on the other. There is also a romanticized notion of a "virtual community" in some aspects of this mothers' movement. Moreover, motherhood can be represented as a problem to be resolved by escaping its demands, while paradoxically celebrating it as an exhilarating new identity. To some extent, an uncoupling occurs between the cultural identity of motherhood and the everyday care of babies and children.

In a discussion of the largely online "newly generated maternalism," Naomi Mezey and Cornelia Pillard view this recent phenomenon with great suspicion. They see the Internet as the engine of "maternalism's rebirth" and as a vehicle for culturally reproducing an image of mothers as happily domestic, "sassy and empowered."[28] In a persuasive analysis of the site Moms Rising, they make some penetrating observations about motherhood as an identity, the infantalization of women in the group's visuals and animations, ambiguous expressions of the desire to act collectively, the use of irony, and the limitations of the organization's reformist politics. However, their main criticism of this so-called new maternalism revolves around what they perceive to be the exclusion of men from the project. This is an important observation, difficult to contest without a comprehensive survey of references to fathers in these emerging Web-based groups. Yet, in promoting "parenting" as a preferable gender-neutral term, the authors risk erasing mothers as a social category altogether. Motherhood is reduced to an individualized private identity. Moreover, neutral terms for care hide gendered patterns of inequality that groups like Moms Rising are perhaps trying to make visible, such as the disproportionate caring labor of women. A more thoroughgoing critique would focus on mothering as a "practice" in which both women and men can engage.

Nevertheless, this attention to or focus on identity rather than on mothering as a practice is a particular limitation of some branches of the mother's movement. Take, for example, the commodification promoted through organizations such as Mamapalooza, which describes itself as a "mom-owned and operated multimedia organization."[29] Its Museum of Motherhood is depicted as "a real and virtual social change museum focused on amplifying the voices and experiences of mothers while connecting 'the cultural family.'"[30] My point here is not to dismiss such developments but to tease out some of the implications of portraying motherhood as somehow an autonomous identity. As Sara Ruddick argued in *Maternal Thinking*, distinctive practices and practice-based forms of reasoning emerge in response to the caring required to preserve the lives of vulnerable children.[31] A compelling conversation between Sara Ruddick and Andrea O'Reilly, founder of the Association for Research on Mothering (now the Motherhood Initiative for Research and Community Involvement), advocate for motherhood studies, and distinguished scholar of feminist mothering, throws considerable light on this area. Ruddick reflects on her ideas at the twentieth anniversary of the publication of *Maternal Thinking*. She compares mothering as a practice to other socially organized practices. "By contrast, some practices are virtually ubiquitous; there is something suspicious about their apparent absence. Mothering is such a practice. This is not because adult humans are inherently motherly but because human children are inherently vulnerable in ways that demand what we call 'mothering.'"[32] Ruddick returns to this theme with O'Reilly. She underlines the fact that mothering (whether it is done by women or men) cannot be separated from the practices of nurturing a child. While nurture is unlinked from instinct and connected instead to cognitive processes, it cannot be split from what Maureen Linker calls "the moral decision making which can occur in the context of a loving relationship between two unequal partners."[33] Ruddick reminds us of the nature of this relationship: "All children are vulnerable. No matter how privileged their social circumstances and blessed by their natural surroundings, children are small, powerless, imperfectly made, subject to illness and abuse. They demand protection. No matter how perspicuous their social circumstance and neurobiological origins and conditions, children's development is complex and subject to many distortions and inhibitions. It demands nurturance."[34] The complexity of children's development and their demand for nurturance can be overlooked in some online groups around motherhood. Not surprisingly, it is difficult to generalize about such diverse activist networks where alliances and membership overlap from group to group and also differ so markedly. Perhaps one of the most paradoxical of these organizations is the Motherhood Project with its "A Call to a Motherhood Movement" manifesto. This movement was, until recently, housed under the auspices of the Institute for American Values. I am aware of the controversial nature of this institute and should note that, from an Australian or European perspective, the emergence of an institute that promoted "Australian," "French," or "British" values would be cause for great suspicion from anyone sensitive to the diversity and multicultural character of most contemporary societies. Also, at the time of writing this, the online presence of the Motherhood Project and its related organization, Watch Out for Children, has mysteriously disappeared from online view.[35] It may be that these Web links are in the process of being renewed. On the other hand, perhaps the Institute for American values has changed its focus on motherhood and there has been a split between the institute and its affiliated scholars and the small group of women from culturally diverse backgrounds who formed its Mothers' Council. Given that I can only speculate about this development, I will rely for my comments about the Motherhood Project on Judith Stadtman Tucker's article "Motherhood and Its Discontents"

and an illuminating interview between Tucker and Enola G. Aird reproduced on the Mothers Movement Online.[36]

Enola G. Aird established and directed the Motherhood Project and
convened the Institute of American Values Mothers' Council. In a 2003
interview, she outlined the aim of the project as providing intellectual
resources and opportunities for exchange to "help spark a mothers'
renaissance." She called for "fresh, creative thinking about the potential,
possibilities, and power of the community of mothers."[37] When questioned on the child-centered focus of the project, she refuted the idea
that there would be a necessary conflict between mothers' rights and
children's needs:

> *The Motherhood Project* wants to point to something admittedly harder
> (but ultimately, bolder and grander), that recognizes the interconnect-
> edness of mothers and children and members of families, and seeks
> to recalibrate the values and priorities of our society so that mothers,
> children, and families get all that they need in order to flourish . . .
>
> We want to create a movement that goes beyond the "work and
> family" debate to a more far-reaching "culture and family" debate. We
> want to see our culture transformed so that the values that currently
> dominate our lives—radical individualism, relentless competition,
> and materialism—yield enough room for the values necessary for
> nurturing human beings and developing human relationships, values
> such as caring, nurturing, and connectedness.[38]

In this interview, Aird also challenged the accepted division between
feminism and maternalism, using as an example the success of early
twentieth-century American maternalist reformers and their advocacy
for women's rights. She outlined a consciously maternalist framework
suited to the complexities of the twenty-first century. The conflict she
identifies is not between feminism and maternalism but rather between
motherhood and the unregulated market (typified by the commercialization of children's lives), rampant consumerism, and a shallow

work-centered culture. The aims of the Motherhood Project are described in communitarian language (see chapter 3) and encourage engaged citizenship and a lively civil society based around family and community.

Despite Aird's refusal to pit maternalism against feminism, the Motherhood Project has often been characterized negatively as being in conflict with the ongoing struggle for women's equality. According to Tucker, the movement fails to confront the dominant ideology of motherhood and supports "the institution of intensive motherhood."[39] Tucker's criticisms go further to include the charge that this particular movement has to abandon "once and for all, the ideal of social and economic equality for women who mother" in order to win its fight for different American values.[40] What is of note here is the discomfort that seems to arise in response to the kind of maternal thinking that places the growth and nurturance of children at the center of any moral reasoning or questions about justice. While my reservations about the Motherhood Project will be developed later, it is almost as though new online expressions of maternalism are acceptable only if certain cultural tenets remain unchallenged. Maternal identity can be rebranded as "empowering," but not if it is viewed as too child-focused or too linked to gender (a focus of my conclusion).

The charge of "intensive mothering," has become part of popular discourse. It operates as a convenient shorthand for mothers who are seen to "care too much." It has also come to represent both a traditional idea of "stay-at-home" motherhood and, at the same time, an apparently new development, where mothers, either working or at home, subject their children to a feverish regime of reading, extension programs, ballet, music, and other forms of "enrichment." Following Sharon Hays's formulation of this phenomenon in *The Cultural Contradictions of Motherhood*, intensive mothering is a method of child rearing that is "child-centered, expert-guided, emotionally absorbing, labor intensive, and financially expensive."[41] A crucial and controversial ingredient in this mix is that mothering is regarded as more important than a mother's paid work.[42] The nuances of Hays's analysis of the discrepancy between this supposedly new ideology of maternal selflessness and wider norms promoting self-interest and a work-centered culture are ignored in the popular usage of term. The term more often is used pejoratively, with little sympathy for mothers who may be caught in this dilemma. The charge of "intensive mothering" is employed to dismiss maternal attentiveness and nurture that is seen as excessive in a culture anxious about care and dependency. In short, the accusation directed against women who are seen to intensively mother can be viewed as another public repudiation of maternalism, what I have been calling postmaternal thinking. The fact that groups in the online mothers' movement charge others with "intensive mothering" (as Tucker does of the Motherhood Project) is another contradictory and unconstructive development.

Sara Ruddick provides the most incisive commentary on how the idea of intensive motherhood has come to be used as a slur. Reflecting on her own critique of the term in the past, Ruddick recalls how at the time she felt it overlapped with what she positively called "fostering growth." She saw the charge of intensive mothering as blaming mothers for "something rotten in culture and state."[43] She relates this to the notion of "momism," sharing her memories with O'Reilly in the conversation already discussed: "But I can't forget the first misogynists who called mothers 'Momists.' These mothers were not so unlike intensive mothers as you have described them. They spent too much time with their children, loved them too much, paid them too much attention, and made them unfit for killing."[44] By actively remembering the history of the term *momism* and its use as an attack on American mothers in the 1940s, Ruddick creates a different view of intensive mothering and the related idea of a "new momism." Susan Douglas and Meredith Michaels develop the notion of the new momism in their popular and irreverent book *The Mommy Myth: The Idealization of Motherhood and How It Has Undermined All Women*. In an oft-cited passage from their introduction, they describe this phenomenon as "the insistence that no woman is truly complete or fulfilled unless she has kids, that women remain the best primary caretakers of children, and that to be a remotely decent mother, a woman has to devote her entire physical, psychological, emotional, and intellectual being, 24/7, to her children. The new momism is a highly romanticized and yet demanding view of motherhood in which the standards for success are impossible to meet."[45] Douglas and Michaels also make reference to the roots of the original term *momism* and seek to "rip it from its misogynistic origins."[46] They attempt to reclaim the term in order to analyze and depict what they view as an essentially media-based ideology. However, the kind of reclamation that Douglas and Michaels envisage is only possible by forgetting the hatred and denunciation of mothers that was both reflected and promoted in the original idea of momism. Mothers at the time were specifically blamed for raising enfeebled (read "homosexual") boys who would be unable to fight for their country.[47] Unlike Ruddick, who strongly contests the term by remembering its nationalist and military associations, Douglas and Michaels fail to sufficiently recast this problematic conception. The pejorative and pervasive use of terms such as *new momism* or *intensive mothering* in popular discourse provide stark evidence that it has not been purged of its offensive mother-hating character.

In the activist groups that constitute the new mothers' movement, these terms are debated and critiqued as well as reproduced. In academic forums and conferences (where the popular and scholarly can overlap), a more critical analysis has been advanced.[48] Andrea O'Reilly, who has pioneered much recent work on feminist mothering, puts forward an alternative notion revolving around concern for children who may be raised with expectations of hyperproductivity and perfectionism. In her conversation with Sara Ruddick she discusses "responsive mothering" as an alternative to intensive mothering that is less market driven, less class based, and more in keeping with maternal thinking.[49] Her dialogue with Ruddick is rich with insights into the risks and dangers of holding mothers responsible for all manner of social ills. It is not possible to do justice to the subtlety of their respective analyses here. However, two aspects of this exchange will frame what is to follow. Both concern propositions made by Ruddick. First, the question of mothering and nonviolence, evident in Ruddick's disgust at the way momism was historically conceived as unpatriotic and as leading to pacificism. Second, the projection onto mothers of what Ruddick calls "something rotten in culture and state."[50] Examining these areas further illuminates some of the ways maternalism has been reconfigured for contemporary purposes.

UNFIT TO KILL   Little Lame Prince

It would be difficult to discuss maternal thinking as an idea and *Maternal Thinking* as an influential text without reference to the subtitle of Ruddick's book: *Toward a Politics of Peace*. While scholarly attention has focused more on the features of maternal thinking than on the link between maternal practice and nonviolence, the latter is crucial to Ruddick's analysis. In the edited collection published to mark the twentieth anniversary of *Maternal Thinking* in 2009, the subtitle of *Philosophy, Politics, Practice* makes no reference to peace. Nevertheless, four of the seventeen essays explicitly concern themselves with maternal thinking as a concept that opens up questions about war and violence.[51] Importantly, this includes Ruddick's own contribution to the collection in her concluding chapter, "Epilogue and a New Beginning."[52] While this epilogue attempts to understand the ideals of maternal nonviolence, Ruddick also discusses feminist peace politics as a practice. Her analysis revolves around the German printmaker and sculptor Käthe Kollwitz and the "feminist pacifism" she advanced following World War I. It is notable that Kollwitz's bronze sculpture of a mother cradling her dead child in her lap now stands in replica in Berlin as a powerful monument to all victims of political oppression and war.[53] Personally speaking, it is impossible to stand before this sculpture and not be stirred by its compassionate embrace and the maternal grief it depicts. It is a monument entirely devoid of nationalist connotations, signaling a more universal ethos of preservative love, care, and protection.

To return briefly to the conclusion in the anniversary collection *Maternal Thinking: Philosophy, Politics, Practice,* Ruddick creatively imagines a link between Kollwitz and the seed planting of Wangari Maathai, the founder of the Green Belt Movement in Kenya. Hence the reference to a new beginning: a complex contemporary interweaving of maternal thinking, peace, and care for the environment. This compelling formulation will be discussed in detail in the next chapter.

One of the most controversial features of the original *Maternal Thinking* has been Ruddick's philosophical approach to the politics of peace. Critics reacted to a perceived connection between male abstract reasoning and war, on the one hand, and maternal concerns and peace on the other. However, such unreflective distinctions are not reproduced in Ruddick's own analysis. Her musings on the nature of war and violence are replete with cautions against such thinking. Women's peacefulness is described as being "at least as mythical as men's violence," and a "pure maternal peacefulness" is declared not to exist.[54] "Although mothers are not intrinsically peaceful," Ruddick asserts, "maternal practice is a 'natural resource' for peace politics" (157). Once again, the key here is Ruddick's notion of practice. The contradiction between mothering and war is revealed when "maternal thinking takes upon itself the critical perspective of a feminist standpoint" (148). She sees discrete motives for rejecting war as arising directly (but not inevitably) from the practice of mothering. The maternal experience of resolving conflict nonviolently also provides a unique perspective from which to criticize military thinking. This view is further elaborated in a passage that adds to the expansive and antiauthoritarian nature of the idea of maternal thinking. It is worth quoting at length for its poetic force, contemporary resonance, and relevance to the discussion to follow.

The analytical fictions of just-war theory require a closure of moral issues final enough to justify killing and "enemies" abstract enough to be killable. In order to welcome their own and their children's changes, mothers have become accustomed to open-ended, concrete reflection on intricate and unpredictable spirits. Maternal attentive love, restrained and clear sighted, is ill adapted to intrusive, let alone murderous, judgments of others' lives. If they have made training a work of conscience and proper trust a virtue, if they have resisted the temptation to dominate their children and abrogate their authority, then mothers have been preparing themselves for patient and conscientious nonviolence, not for the obedience and excessive trust in authority on which military adventures thrive.

(150)

Elsewhere, the political dimensions of maternal attentive love come to the fore. In her "Preliminary Note About Peace" and in the last chapters of *Maternal Thinking*, Ruddick attempts to introduce a much more active, robust definition of peace. The aim is to move toward an understanding of what "peace might look like," and one source can be found in the peacefulness of nonviolent activism. This is distinguished from pacifism. It is an activism Ruddick sees as latent in maternal practice. In her own words: "It is the peacefulness of nonviolent activism to which I hope mothers, along with other women and men, can contribute" (137).

Is Ruddick's hope realized in the activism of the contemporary mothers' movement? One could argue that it is both enacted and disowned. As an example of the latter, it is important to return to the Motherhood Project. It is remarkable to see a reuse of just-war theory in this group's commitment to war in Iraq and Afghanistan. Disturbingly, the language of maternalism is one idiom through which this commitment is expressed. In 2002, for example, a letter was published that outlined the "moral reasoning" behind the Institute for American Values support for war. Enola Aird, founder of the Motherhood Project, and other prominent intellectuals, lawyers, religious leaders, and public figures were the signatories to the letter, "What We're Fighting For: A Letter from America."[55] The letter mounts the same critique of American society used by the Motherhood Project, namely, rampant consumerism, self-seeking individualism, and the decline of community. Ironically, this same critique formed the basis for the call for a mothers' renaissance to promote entirely different values of caring, nurture, and connectedness. However, in this case, these values are invoked to justify war through the maternal desire to "protect the innocent from certain harm."[56] It is possible that at the time of the letter's publication the participants in this group may have had an independent view on the war from that of the Institute for American Values. I do not wish to misrepresent them here or conflate their views. However, given the key role of the founder, Enola Aird, the letter raises questions about the extent to which maternalism has been actually reconfigured in the contemporary mothers' movement or conventionally framed in the same narrow nationalist terms as the maternalism of the past.

While the Motherhood Project is certainly not representative of the mothers' movement as a whole, it does stand in stark contrast to Ruddick's analysis of the connection between maternal practice and peace. Of course, there are countless historical examples of mothers mobilizing for violent and nationalist causes, as Ruddick herself acknowledges.[57] Many of these examples have been used to critique *Maternal Thinking* and, in particular, what is perceived to be its normalizing notion of preservative love.[58] In the case of Enola Aird's group, it seems that preservative love cannot be extended across national boundaries to the children of Iraq and Afghanistan. However, the point of my examination here is to pose different kinds of questions. How can new meanings of maternalism be configured to suit the current global geopolitical context if nationalist concerns remain predominant? Is it possible to create alternative notions of maternal citizenship that resist historical constructions of women as Mothers of the Nation? Are there contemporary forms of maternalism that are founded on a politics that is antistate and transnational? Are there movements, as Ruddick envisaged, where maternal thinking is the philosophical foundation of a feminist peace politics for the twenty-first century?

There are two recent examples of nonviolent activism that throw some light on these questions. Both attempt to translate symbols of mothering into political speech about the injustice of war. The first,

CODEPINK, calls on mothers, grandmothers, sisters and daughters and women all around the world "to rise up and oppose the war in Iraq," to stop new wars and redirect energy into healthcare "green jobs and other life affirming activities."[59] While also inviting men to join the movement, CODEPINK outlines its focus in maternalist terms: "Women have been the guardians of life—not because we are better or purer or more innately nurturing than men, but because the men have busied themselves making war. Because of our responsibility to the next generation, because of our own love for our families and communities and this country that we are a part of, we understand the love of a mother in Iraq for her children, and the driving desire of that child for life."[60] As a global social movement, CODEPINK uses new mobilizing strategies and online forms of activism similar to those of other contemporary global networks. Old and new tactics are creatively combined. Members (dressed in pink) protest at rallies and demonstrations, engage in street theater, and disrupt congressional hearings. They also promote their campaigns and antics via a strong Internet presence and on YouTube. Members receive regular "activist alerts" that cover a wide range of issues. For instance, at the time of writing, CODEPINK members were urged to send e-cards to conservative family members, friends, colleagues to show how "the war economy does not leave us with enough of the pie to feed our families."[61] The group also targeted Tea Party members on Tax Day (April 13, 2010) who were protesting big government and supporting lower taxes. Code Pink's aim was to reveal what they called "the biggest sinkhole" of tax dollars, namely, military spending. The movement professes members that cross the political spectrum, differ in class constitution, and come from diverse cultural backgrounds. They also promote "joy and humor" in their approach to peace activism and aim to move beyond the grim seriousness and moralizing of earlier peace movements. This antidisciplinary attitude to protest is another significant feature of new transnational movements and networks demonstrated by CODEPINK.[62]

In an instructive analysis of Code Pink and related peace campaigns, Kristin Goss and Michael Heaney view such movements as notable for their unconventional modes of organizing and the challenges they pose to the ways women's collective action has conventionally been framed.[63] Like Ruddick, the authors acknowledge the long history of women at the vanguard of antiviolence movements. Starting with the Woman's Peace Party in World War 1, moving onto Women's Action Against Nuclear Disarmament during the cold war and the Women Against Gun Violence campaigns in the 1990s, they document activism spanning nearly a century.[64] While the authors' examples relate only to the United States, a more global perspective might also include the Women's Peace Army founded in Australia in 1915, the Greenham Common Women's Peace Camp in Berkshire, England to oppose the nuclear weapons facility there in the 1980s, or the more recent International Human Rights March of Women through Israel and Palestine. The list would be endless. However, Goss and Heaney make a strong case that groups like CODEPINK "are worthy of attention not only because of the vibrancy of their organizing, but also because of their substantive focus. They have addressed entrenched, non-gender specific public issues during an era in which much of women's organizational energy has gravitated to narrower issues of women's rights and status."[65] The authors argue that the hybrid character of CODEPINK is the factor that enables the group's success. They identify three frames that creatively intermingle in CODEPINK's activism: the maternal frame, the equality frame, and the feminine-expressive frame. It is the combination of maternalism and egalitarianism that is of particular interest to the question of how a feminist maternalism could be reconceptualized to face the challenges of the current period.

Goss and Heaney argue that in CODEPINK and antiviolence campaigns such as the Million Mom March for gun control (May 2000), the historical tension between ideas of women's care ethic on the one hand and a rights-based analysis on the other are imaginatively resolved. They provide detailed empirical evidence to support the view that these groups successfully attract a wide range of participants at a time when there is an absence of a clear consensus among women about what unites them.[66] Using social movement theory as the framework, the authors show how the discourses of maternalism and egalitarianism are synthesized in a way that does not alienate women who identify more with one perspective rather than the other. Their analysis of the expressive components in these new forms of activism is instructive and notable. Exaggerated gendered symbols of motherhood or female sexuality (pink slips and underwear) are employed in parodic, playful ways when marching in the streets or confronting opponents. These expressive elements create what the authors call "maternalism with a wink" and "traditional femininity with a wink." Perhaps this expressive politics holds a key to one of the ways maternalism could be reshaped. It is notable how many groups in the mothers' movements so far discussed in this chapter take a traditional symbol, such as Mother's Day, and transform its meaning in order to politicize issues relevant to mothers and children. The paradox, of course, is that, in the very period when gender-neutral perspectives dominated public discussion, the use of heightened gendered symbols seems to unite rather than divide women activists. This is a point I will develop in the concluding chapter.

The second contemporary case of the maternal being made political in order to oppose war is that of Cindy Sheehan, whose peace activism has directly arisen from her experiences and practices as a mother. When Sheehan's own son was killed in Iraq in 2004, she began speaking out against the war and mobilizing with other peace organizations. Facing rejection from her husband, family members, and some sections of the media, Sheehan made it her mission to hold the then U.S. president, George W. Bush, accountable for the Iraq war. As a grieving mother, and using language that was visceral and unsettling, Sheehan transformed a traditional, concrete maternal perspective into political speech. Her public utterances employ vividly maternalist images of war as always fought with "our babies' blood" or of the "blood-monied devils" of the Bush regime who shouldn't be able to look their children and grandchildren in the eye. "How does it feel that the vultures are laughing at how gullible we are to so naively cough up our young? Previous generations of mothers have watched presidents and other cheerleaders for war and mayhem drag us into war after war and we mothers are unwilling and unknowing accomplices in our children's murders."[67]

Sheehan's use of direct actions such as picketing, marching, lobbying, setting up peace camps in Texas near the ranch of the George W. Bush, media campaigns, and hunger strikes have been constant since the death of her son. Arrested numerous times, including as recently as March 2010, Sheehan argues in favor of mothers "putting their bodies on the line to stop war." She attributes her own fearlessness to the fact that "when you bury a child, there is nothing worse that can happen to you. I don't have anything else to lose." In an essay by Linda Pershing, the links between Sheehan's perspective and Ruddick's notion of maternal thinking are persuasively made. Pershing bases her analysis on participant observation of Sheehan at various peace encampments and political actions and also on Sheehan's own writings. In giving a personal dimension to the essay, Pershing discusses how she had no real connection to the war in Iraq until she heard about Sheehan. She writes: "Her son Casey, just three years older than my daughter, had been murdered by a bullet to the head. My immediate reaction stemmed from my experiences as a mother. I felt empathy for Sheehan, and I was excited by the attempt to hold the president—whose two children would never enlist in the military—accountable."[68] These comments demonstrate the success of Sheehan's maternalist strategies. Where it would be possible to see only differences (note that Pershing has a daughter, not a son, her daughter is three years older, and the family is highly educated with leftist politics), Sheehan's plea appeals to maternal subjectivity as a universal condition, so only the similarities become important. A final strikingly maternalist element in Sheehan's peace activism is her use of the term *matriotism*. According to Sheehan, matriots are people who love their country but will oppose their country if it is "murdering thousands upon thousands" of innocent humans. The term is given a strongly internationalist inflection by Sheehan, who comments: "War will end forever when we Matriots stand up and say: 'No, I am not giving up my child to the fake patriotism of the war machine, which chews up my flesh and blood to spit out obscene profits.'"[69]

In an important empirical study of contemporary women's antiwar and antimilitary peace organizations worldwide, Cynthia Cockburn provides persuasive evidence of what she describes as the feminist consciousness that often arises from "close encounters with militarization and war."[70] Significantly, she returns to feminist standpoint theory (also employed by Ruddick twenty-one years earlier) as a generative framework from which to understand women's peace activism. The "feminism" that Cockburn unearths in her research is both "extraordinarily holistic" and, by definition, "transnational."[71] In a related article Cockburn provides examples from Japan and South Korea to show that what marks feminist peace activism as different is its attention to "more mundane violence and the individual lives it affects, to pain, care and responsibility."[72] In the case of the South Korean organization, Women Making Peace, the aim is to develop and promote a widespread "peace culture" that transforms oppressive gender relations. The emphasis in these organizations on relationships of care and nonviolence brings maternalism once again into focus.

Such campaigns and movements, like CODEPINK or the activism of Cindy Sheehan, signal the possibility of unlinking maternalism from nationalism and developing quite different political configurations around peace, nurture, and care. A new maternalism would encompass distinctive kinds of maternal subjectivities and refuse the Mothers of the Nation label. A focus on what Alison Bailey calls "the political and epistemic implications of maternal work" may open up spaces for transnational dialogues that go far beyond the narrow ideological frameworks associated with the maternalism of the past.[73]

THE MATERNAL AND POSTMATERNAL IN TENSION

Any discussion of a new maternal politics would have to include reference to the collection of essays in *The Maternal Is Political: Women Writers at the Intersection of Motherhood and Social Change*, a text widely cited in online discussions and often connected to the new mothers' movement. Edited by Shari MacDonald Strong, author, blogger, and founder of the Web-based magazine *Literary Mama,* the collection is introduced with an impassioned appeal for mothers to give voice to the issues concerning them in order to empower themselves. Strong urges everyone, regardless of their gender, if they are parents or if child free, to "Vote Mother."[74] What this may mean is unclear, particularly given that there is no direct call for political action in this text. An oblique general reference is made to the fact that no administration would be able to "stand up to *all* the mothers."[75] Even though this is an uneven and at times puzzling collection, it is relevant to our discussion because of its claim to politicize the maternal. The book covers an enormous range of topics and contributors. For instance, writing is included by the late Benazir Bhutto, former prime minister of Pakistan, from a 1997 article about spending some time with her children. This rather odd piece is included, one assumes, because Bhutto was a mother in a political role. That writing contrasts with various everyday musings on maternal mental health, mothers returning to study, or Rebecca Walker's battling with issues of organic food, pesticides, and cancer-fighting agents in the home in an effort to create a healthy environment for her son.[76] All contributions are in the form of short, personal narratives, with little attempt to link these diverse reflections. In keeping with some aspects of the online mothers' movement covered so far, motherhood features at times as an identity rather than as a relationship with a child or children.

Before arguing that this collection signals some of the limitations and problems of producing new meanings around the maternal, a brief examination of the contribution by Cindy Sheehan is in order. In contrast to the fierce "matriotism" and its connection to peace activism previously identified, Sheehan "resigns" from politics in this essay, "Good Riddance, Attention Whore."[77] Notes reveal that this intervention was written in 2007. Yet to date it is clear that Sheehan has not resigned and continues her tireless campaigns for peace. This is evident in the fact that Sheehan characteristically marked Mother's Day 2010 with a radio speech about war and profiteering.[78] By contrast, her contribution to *The Maternal Is Political* uses a different voice, in this case that of a weary, disillusioned former activist. The essay revolves around Sheehan's revelation that her son Casey died for nothing.[79] She describes her failed efforts to make her son's sacrifice meaningful and lists the personal toll her activism has taken from public abuse, health and hospital bills, factionalism in the peace movement, and endless and offensive labeling by the media. She expresses her desire to "go home and be a mother to her surviving children."[80] While this essay could be read as disingenuous, an artful plea for others to act against war (as indicated by her final call: "It's up to you now"),[81] it also embodies the tensions between maternalism as a public stance and the maternal as a private condition based on the preservation of particular children's lives. This tension is implicit in other contributions but is writ large by Sheehan in her longing to eschew politics and devote herself to her surviving children. In this respect, the expansion of contemporary maternal forms of subjectivity to a universal ethic of care can be viewed as a fragile basis for political citizenship, as critics of maternalism have long argued.

Another tension between the public and private is evident in the troubling contribution by Sarah Masterson, author of a resource handbook for expectant and new parents in Washington called *D.C. Baby*. In her narrative, "Alien," the author extols the virtues of her Bolivian maid and nanny, Mimi.[82] Masterson provides her own narrative about Mimi's life, imagining her burying her face in her then three-year-old daughter's hair in Bolivia before heading for America. Masterson is confident that Mimi's motherhood is the reason she came to Washington and is also the reason she stays. "She came as a mother, and she stays because she is a mother—though she hasn't buried her face in Adrianna's [her daughter's] dark curls for more than a decade, and may not for years to come" (26). This disturbing prediction is followed by a long list of the nurturing—the preservative love—Mimi performs for the author's own three-year-old American daughter, Ava. This inventory includes all the maternal tasks, practical, social, and ethical: rocking Ava to sleep, wiping her tears, feeding her, vigilantly protecting her, teaching her the colors of the American flag and the name of the president, and showing her how to be "strong and kind and brave" (27). However, Mimi has another task in addition to all the others she performs. She also nurtures Masterson, bringing her cake on Mother's Day, holding her face in her hands and kissing her, becoming a mother to the mother of the child she is paid to care for.

Ostensibly this is an essay criticizing the gap between what is legal in the United States and what is moral. Mimi is a so-called illegal alien, and Masterson would like her to be able to have a proper legal status so she could go home to visit her daughter in Bolivia but "return to the working life that is supporting her daughter" (28). Notably, Masterson does not call, at first, for a political change that would allow full citizenship for Mimi and her family, where Mimi's daughter Adrianna could live with her mother legally in America. Such a position would raise an obvious conflict: who would look after Masterson's daughter, Ava? So what is presented here is a profoundly contradictory maternalist position. Masterson depicts her own motherhood as entitling her to a political language and universalizes Mimi, on the one hand, as "every mother," while, on the other, she particularizes Mimi as her own mother. As Masterson puts it:

Only when I saw myself in Mimi's dark and resilient eyes could I know how and why my government is getting it all wrong.

I'd like to worry less about what the future holds for Mimi if we can't afford her, or if we outgrow the need for full-time childcare. I'd like not to think about what it would mean for my daughter to lose this woman she has no memory of ever having lived without. Because Mimi is not just an employee. She is my mother. She is me.

(28–29)

This strange blend of individualism, maternalism, narcissism, and romanticism is an uncomfortable mix. Regrettably, it is not unusual. It is a familiar response to the deep discomfort produced by the introduction of market relations into the home. The point here is not an individual one about Masterson's narrative, but a general reflection on the limits of a certain form of maternalist politics.

Blurred distinctions about what is considered to be "work" and what constitutes "care" are central to this politics. The high demand for and recruitment of immigrant female domestic labor in the U.S., the UK, and Europe is based precisely on this perceived lack of clarity in the distinction between work and care. Market relations are disguised, particularly where intimate care in the home is concerned. This point is developed in a range of significant and politically engaged scholarship. Different scholars strive to make visible the power dynamics in this sector.[83] Others, including documentary filmmakers, expose the "ideological and structural forces that maintain domestic work as a poorly paid and undervalued racial, gendered, class-based and increasingly transnational labor practice."[84] A recent U.S. survey conducted by Domestic Workers United found that 98 percent of domestic workers are foreign born and 59 percent are the primary income earners for their families.[85] In a powerful article, "A Very Private Business: Explaining the Demand for Migrant Domestic Workers," Bridget Anderson records remarkably uniform perceptions about the ability of women from different nationalities to be caring, warm, docile, natural housekeepers, or happy.[86] She bases her detailed observations on two comprehensive empirical studies including a four-country pilot study that surveyed employers of immigrant domestic workers. In-depth interviews were conducted with employers of live-in and live-out domestic workers, staff at agencies, support organizations, and different advocacy groups. General observations about national characteristics and perceived cultural facilities to "protect" and "nurture" were shown to shape employer and, consequently, market preferences. However, there is profound disquiet at defining the relationship between employer and domestic worker in market terms. This is particularly so when a white, middle-class mother pays another mother from an impoverished, immigrant background to care for the employer's children rather than her own. Take, for example, these comments from an employer quoted by Anderson. "I really feel strongly that it's a positive thing you can do for somebody . . . I think it's liberating for a girl from the Philippines to . . . leave the rice paddy fields and the village and to be able to send back huge amounts of money and to be able to get a job in England."[87] Complex cultural constructions about the special and purportedly "natural" caring abilities of the domestic worker serve an obvious pragmatic purpose and also create the illusion that the relationship is one of mutual dependence. In Anderson's persuasive words, "power is clothed in the language of obligation, support and responsibility, rather than power and exploitation."[88] Note that this intermingling of idioms of kinship and mutuality can also be observed in Masterson's comments about her maid and nanny Mimi as being both her mother and her own self.

Barbara Ehrenreich and Arlie Russell Hochschild, in their edited collection *Global Woman: Nannies, Maids, and Sex Workers in the New Economy*, would describe the situation of Mimi from Bolivia as a part of a "global care chain."[89] This is a system of caretaking where poor women leave home to go to another country to care for someone else's children, while depending on other family members (or local domestic workers) in their own country to care for their children. Hochschild would also identify this as a global care "drain." This is defined as a one-way transfer of emotional labor, where the love and care usually provided by women to the young, the old, and the sick in their own poor countries is transferred to the young, the old, and the sick in rich countries, whether as maids, nannies, or day care and nursing home aides.[90] Yet mothers employing such home-based domestic labor depict this transfer in far from commercial terms. As one mother, described as an "American lawyer," comments: "Carmen just enjoys my son. She doesn't worry whether . . . he's learning his letters, or whether he'll get into a good preschool. She just enjoys him. And actually with anxious, busy parents like us, that is what Thomas really needs. I love my son more than anything in this world. But at this stage, Carmen is better for him."[91]

Is this time-poor professional lawyer suggesting that a "surrogate" mother, who is paid for her time, can offer her son more than she can? Hochschild is unambiguous about the cost of globalization for the biological children of paid live-in nannies and carers such as Carmen or Mimi. She views it as a clear breach of Article 9 of the United Nations Declaration on the Rights of the Child, which pledges that children should not be "separated from [their] parents against their will."[92] However, the comments by the mother employing Carmen also reveal a great deal about contemporary understandings of care and work in a neoliberal context. They bring back into sharp focus what I have called postmaternal thinking and its relationship to feminism and cultural memory.

Where does feminism feature in configurations of care that include the commodification of mothering, love, and nurture? Is there a process of cultural forgetting that eases discomfort about "the commercialization of intimate life," to use Hochschild's evocative words? And what ideological and cultural formations assist in so concealing issues of power and exploitation? The mother and "American lawyer" quoted by Ehrenreich and Hochschild depicts her maid and nanny as being able to "just enjoy" the lawyer's son, Thomas. This enjoyment is measured by the fact that Carmen is not worrying about Thomas learning the alphabet or competing for the best preschool. These concerns are portrayed as being both the domain and the entitlement of the parents. They are somehow prevented from just enjoying their son, by virtue of their busyness and their anxieties about Thomas's future academic performance. They are also constrained by a sense that they (and people like them) have lost the ability to care in this more "natural" way. Carmen's labor creates the time for the parents to work and the space for them to worry about how best to maximize their income as well as their son's potential in areas with market value.

The scenario played out in microcosm here between the American lawyer mother and the immigrant nanny is one where nurture and care have been resignified. Unconditional love is outsourced. There is the implication that such emotions are best found, if not *only* found, offshore, in immigrant women who are seen to have come from "more family oriented cultures." It is as though these emotions (and abilities) still reside in cultures where significant proportions of the population are not fully integrated into a capitalist, individualized, work-centered economy. The corollary is the perception that the ability to simply nurture and enjoy children has, one way or another, been lost or made extremely complicated in advanced capitalist societies where women are pictured (and picture themselves) in equally possessive individualist terms to men. If women are imagined in these terms, a different language of care is used. Care is reframed as enrichment, responsibility, risk, worrisome, and, significantly, a burden to be managed efficiently. These terms highlight the way the distinctions between work and home have not only been blurred but serve, as they always have done, important practical and ideological purposes.

Complex processes of cultural forgetting underpin new cultural conceptions around what it means to nurture a child. Supposedly old meanings are embodied in representations of nannies such as Mimi or Carmen. These meanings are also constructed as having been lost. However, as discussed in preceding chapters and following the work of Paul Connerton, this loss is a patterned and collective procedure working in the interests of the formation of a new identity. There are obvious gains in both forgetting the care these nannies can remember and in forgetting that paid home care involves power and exploitation. The gains of cultural forgetting in this instance are threefold: financial, by freeing up time for mothers to engage in paid work; psychological, by providing the comfort that their children are still getting "uncomplicated" nurture and love; and ideological, by preserving the illusion that the home is separate from the market and governed only by affective relations and ties. Importantly, this cultural forgetting provides a convenient way, at least at the personal level, to reconcile feminist claims for autonomy with the ever present and thorny constraints of human dependency.

To detour for a moment, when it comes to care for children outside the home in day care, this reconciliation is achieved by a different means. References to the affective (the need for loving/nurturing care) are secondary to discourses about maximizing a child's potential. The nostalgia for older forms of nurturing evident in previous comments is not apparent in public expectations about commercial child-care centers. In this respect, the ideal of home remains untouched by market values and becomes the preserve of "uncomplicated" love and nurture. By contrast, in day care, the language of attentive care replaces any references to loving care. This is often illustrated in the way commercial care is marketed. An illuminating example can be found in an Australian corporate child-care chain, ABC Learning, which became the largest child-care chain in the world. The company was the dominant private sector player in the child-care industry in Australia and went bankrupt during the global financial crisis, owing $2 billion to creditors. In a *Sunday Life* newspaper supplement shortly before its collapse, a photograph of an infant and her carer is reproduced to look like the kind of photographs of children and family that parents magnetize to refrigerator doors. The commentary linked to the photograph, purportedly by a happy mother, is revealing.

> I see my two daughters genuinely love learning from their carers. My girls are always coming home with a new skill or song. The ABC carers make learning fun through music and play. We have two very different girls and they both receive the individual attention needed from the ABC staff to help them achieve their own potential. I couldn't be happier with the progress my children are making at ABC. They have become confident, outgoing, and able to handle different social situations and I believe this is largely because of the quality of care they are receiving at ABC.[93]

Aside from the references to skills formation, learning, and social development, what needs to be noted here is that the infant in the photograph called Nicola is described as being eighteen months old! The penetration of neoliberal ideas of productivity to babies and infants is only one disturbing aspect of this example. Another is the normalization of this new social configuration around care. Far from the "preservative love" theorized by Ruddick, this care is measured in outcomes and is all about extending children's competencies. Moreover, when children dutifully perform the skills they acquire, "coming home with a new skill or song," parents are reassured that the care they are getting is "quality" and, of course, value for money.

This is not to simplify the multifaceted and contested subject of commercial child care. In Australia and in other national contexts this is a particularly fraught and divisive issue, possibly because access to child care was one of the key platforms of second-wave feminism. As I have commented elsewhere, certainly in Australia there seems to be a knee-jerk reaction to any social research that questions the benefits of day care for children.[94] Despite dissenting feminist voices, the dominant orthodoxies around this issue seem much more entrenched here than in other similar countries. Undoubtedly, the most far-reaching and sensitive analysis of the whole issue of institutional child care is by social philosopher Anne Manne in her book *Motherhood: How Should We Care for Our Children?*[95] Not only does Manne's study comprehensively review the relevant research findings on the effects of long hours of institutional care on children and the relevant literature on attachment theory, Manne's intervention is distinguished by its child-centered feminist focus. Her analysis covers key policy and gender implications of the "shadow economy of care," but also paves the way for thinking differently about the ethical dimensions of caring for children. She raises questions about selfhood, justice, and moral action and mounts a powerful critique of the penetration of the neoliberal market into everyday life. Manne shares with authors such as Arlie Russell Hochschild a profound unease with "what it means to buy or sell emotional labor." [96]

The high value placed on an increasingly individuated self (perfectly tailored for the demands of the flexible labor market) is strengthened by an acceptance of the need to purchase care through paid consumption. Yet, as the examples discussed in this chapter show, this is never an untroubled or easy acceptance. Nostalgia for premarket relationships, the production of new meanings about what it is to nurture a child, and the reinvigorated maternalism of the new mothers' movement all signal tensions around the neoliberal promise of a productive, autonomous, self-sufficient life of rationality and modernity. It would be true to say that feminism plays a complicated role in both strengthening and challenging this tension. On the one hand, women's move into paid work is promoted as the path to autonomy and, on the other, the market is critiqued as self-interested, inauthentic, and heartless. Importantly, both conceptions fortify imagining "home" as separate from the market and governed by mutual dependence and affective relations. According to Anderson, to imagine these spheres as opposing is actually "mutually reinforcing."[97] However, the idea of the home as a refuge from the unfeeling market can be traced back to early capitalist conceptions of public/private. It is difficult to move beyond taken-for-granted understandings of this binary division. In its contemporary form, this distinction is commonly represented as the work/family divide or the balance between work and home. The dominant language of a *divide,* or split, between the two signals a desire for this distinction to remain intact but minus the conflict. However, the reality, as much of Hochschild's research demonstrates, is a growing interchange between these spheres, and home has come to be perceived as (hard) work, while work is reported as feeling more and more like home. In a personal interview in the *Journal of Consumer Culture*, Hochschild reflects back on the wide empirical research she conducted for her books on this topic. "The people I was interviewing saw 'work–family balance' as a *personal* act. And I saw it that way, at first, too. But I began to see the real issue as a balance, not between personal *roles* but between social—and moral—*worlds*."[98] This idea of social and moral worlds goes beyond current frameworks of understanding and raises trenchant questions about the changing meanings of and shifting emotions around work, home, dependency, and care.

Hochschild further develops these ideas in her essay "'Rent a Mom' and Other Services: Markets, Meaning, and Emotions."[99] She signals some new understandings produced by the paid consumption of emotional services. Using the metaphor of a wall between market and nonmarket life, she shows how, in some contexts, this wall appears fixed, yet, in others, permeable. We may be living, she suggests, on one side of the commercial wall, but our feelings might reside on the other. Alternatively, shifting back and forth across the wall may mean desymbolizing one kind of action as a sign of love—the imperfect but homemade birthday cake, for example — and then resymbolizing the commercial transaction as being the "more loving" option, in this case the purchasing of a "perfect" cake.[100] In my reading of this essay in the light of Hochschild's earlier work, it is clear that certain themes emerge which are relevant to the discussion of the tension between the maternal and the post-maternal and the role of memory in resignifying nurture and care. One constant can be identified in the way Hochschild's subjects talk about their feelings. While affective meanings may shift and change according to the context, and the commercial wall may not have a fixed, agreed upon definition, there remains a determined attachment to nonmarket identities and values. This may emerge as nostalgia, as in the example of the mother paying a live-in nanny to provide the "simple" mothering of yesteryear, or it may surface in discourses about (and a yearning for) what has been forgotten from the past. Memory therefore plays a strong role in the depiction of premarket identities and lives.

This book began with an uneasy reference to a self-help text designed apparently to teach us to remember how to be at ease with a loved one who is gravely ill. Ironically, all manner of market mechanisms exist to retrieve lost memories and rediscover forms of care associated with the past. However, this is neither a direct or uncomplicated process. Some of the complexities and paradoxes in the way memories are made and remade in the home have been identified in the revived scholarly interest in everyday family rituals, narratives, and symbols. According to John R. Gillis, "the past has become the preferred space of the family imaginary."[101] He uses the framework of Marjorie Garber in *Sex and Real Estate: Why We Love Houses* to support the idea that the contemporary family has become like an imagined entity, "the families we wish we could have if only we had the time and the room for them.'[102] Garber notes: "We build exercise rooms instead of exercising, furnish libraries instead of reading, install professional kitchens instead of cooking."[103] Extending this interpretation, families, like homes, have become full of emblems to "that which is absent." Gillis describes this as the increasingly virtual character of contemporary families. In this respect, we have little time to ever really make actual the relationships and affective ties we associate with "home." This is where Hochschild's analysis comes in. Purchasing the material symbols of these ties, in products and services, is, oddly enough, not so much "outsourcing" but bringing "home, back home."[104] Such suggestive observations by Hochschild or Gillis raise questions that extend our understanding of contemporary discomfort around the maternal. Are the new and compelling online expressions of maternalism in mothers' movements, peace activism, and popular texts bringing motherhood "home," back into public view, or reinforcing a virtual quality in the realms of care and nurture? Posing this question may assist in moving toward some tentative conclusions about the possibility of another kind of neomaternalism reconfigured along different feminist lines.

Conclusion
Toward a New Feminist Maternalism

> Just as I reject the labeling of eco/feminist activism
> as essentialist . . . similarly I reject the disavowal of maternalism in
> accounts of eco/feminist activism, or the narrating of
> motherhood as that which needs to be left behind in the past on
> the way to an activist future.
>
> NIAMH MOORE, "Debating Eco/Feminist Natures"

This book began with a discussion of cultural forgetting. It will end with speculation about a form of remembering that has emerged in some feminist responses to the current environmental crisis. I have attempted to advance an idea of postmaternal thinking and its relationship to particular memories of second-wave feminism. By examining some of the different cultural ways motherhood has been narrated, I have tried to theorize contemporary expressions of a profound cultural anxiety around the maternal and more general notions of care, nurture, and dependency. However, there are strong resistances emerging that challenge this postmaternal culture. As always, problems as well as promises are embedded in these challenges, particularly in the reemergence of maternalism in the public domain. So any conclusions about this trend are, by definition, provisional. The larger social and political context that shapes the way memories are made and remade is always dynamic and subject to contest. Given that this is not a policy-oriented investigation, the point has been to open up questions and provide a different lens through which an alternative feminist politics can be imagined.

One guiding question concerns the extent to which dominant renderings of feminism have become degendered. Evidence of gender neutrality can be found in the neoliberal restructuring of social provision of welfare support (such as workfare or welfare to work programs). Returning to Ann Orloff's characterization of this restructuring as "a farewell to maternalism," these policies mark an end of support for women to stay at home to care for children.[1] According to this current policy regime, social rewards are given for paid labor, not unpaid caregiving. As I have proposed in chapter 1, the cultural devaluation of the principles of nurture and care reflected in these changes, and in the market promise of a self-sufficient individualism, are akin to an "unmothering" of society as a whole. Gender neutrality is also the idealized model of the liberal citizen as a permanently competent, genderless adult who possesses "all the requisite capacities for self-government" (see chapter 2).[2] It is hardly surprising, then, that the feminism given most public prominence today is a comprehensively degendered version. While it is true that the second wave was predicated on an analysis of the social meanings and relationships of power and subordination attributed to gender difference, it also aimed to address "gender-blindness." According to Seyla Benhabib, to be blind to gender was to fail to take into account the standpoint, activities, and experiences of women and to be impervious to patterns of thinking and feeling characterized as "female."[3] The theoretical debates around this issue are arcane and multifaceted and not the primary focus of this book. Nevertheless, Benhabib's depiction of standpoint theory in particular does highlight the centrality of gender to any feminist project that aims to give the experiences and activities of women a public presence and legitimacy. Obviously, this is crucial where maternal experiences are concerned.

It would be difficult to be blind to the fact that caregiving activities continue to be thoroughly gendered. Moreover, despite four decades of theorizing and some recognition of the ideological, institutional, and personal dimensions of gender difference, it remains the situation that in most social and cultural contexts the idea that there are two genders is remarkably persistent. Even though there are strong notions of gender-neutrality in the public sphere, it remains clear that in nearly all advanced democracies the paid caring professions such as nursing, child care, or social work continue to be dominated by women. Emotions and activities around care in the private sphere are also gendered. How then can a gender-blind approach achieve just treatment for those engaged in caregiving labor?

Paradoxically, when issues concerning the care of babies and children gain public attention and questions are raised about "family-friendly" models of employment, a degendered version of feminism seems to emerge more forcefully than ever. Take, for example, debates about the possibility of paid leave arrangements for parents after the birth of babies, which I will call baby-leave for reasons that will become clear. Arguments are frequently given prominence that "the parenthood conundrum" should be "articulated in gender-neutral ways."[4] We are urged to agree with the proposition that this is not a "women's issue."[5] The discourse runs that, in the interests of gender equity, the maternal should be written out of the leave equation, once and for all. As an example of a dominant strand of feminism, this gender-equity paradigm is oddly degendered. So too is the conventional model of the contemporary family as dual income and dual carer.[6] One parent is encouraged to take leave and look after the baby in the months after birth so that the other can swiftly return to work. At first glance this seems like an ideal situation. It is portrayed (rightly) as an important step toward emancipating women from an unequal care burden. And few would argue against the social, family, and personal benefits of men being able to access leave to better contribute to the care of their children. Dramatic shifts in conditions around employment and care are long overdue. However, this does not detract from other problems with this model. First, it is a model that perfectly suits the demands of today's workplaces and is closely related to unsustainable patterns of consumption requiring two incomes and significant family indebtedness.

Moreover, the dual career, dual carer model, demands (in its present form) impossibly long working hours and measurements of performance that ultimately devalue children and caring responsibilities. It is not a model that promotes reduced working hours and more part-time work for both men and women. Second, this model fails to address the broader questions raised by Nancy Fraser, in a recent interview, about what exact role should wage labor play in modern society? "How should it relate to care and other forms of social participation?"[7] Thirdly, this model can serve to reproduce notions of care as a transferable and marketable commodity. In a neoliberal context, and with the emphasis on full-time employment, it relies on care being outsourced to the commercial market. This raises the dilemmas of commodification previously covered. Finally, the dual-income, dual-carer model can close off and censor important questions about the specificities of female embodiment.

Clearly, the materiality of embodied motherhood is acutely marked for women after they have given birth. Nowhere is this more evident than in the practice of breastfeeding. In a keynote address at a social policy conference, Ann Orloff briefly made mention of an article in the *New Yorker* by journalist Jill Lepore about the increasing use of the motorized breast pump in the United States today.[8] In my view, this intriguing article highlights the difficult ways that advanced democratic societies in the English-speaking world are struggling with issues of care and human vulnerability. The evidence compiled by Lepore paints a stark and dramatic picture of what I have called postmaternal thinking. Before discussing this article, it is necessary to point out that this is not a rehearsal of the old "breast is best" debate, but rather a forum to ask whether we have moved into a new phase of commodification where mothers' breasts have become harnessed to industrial processes.

According to Lepore, the once unsightly, if not feared medical contraption of the breast pump has become a personal accessory item, designed to look like a Fendi briefcase or a Gucci backpack. New mothers with professional careers in the United States are being offered work-based "lactation rooms" as incentives to return to work as soon as possible after giving birth. Women can make online bookings for the purpose-designed pumping chairs in these rooms, where they can "comfortably" plug in and express milk during a work break. These lactation rooms are presented as evidence of a supposedly caring workplace. So it seems as though the newly developed corporate lactation policies of companies like Goldman Sachs, have become the accepted substitute for maternity leave.[9] Professional women are increasingly describing themselves as "lactating mothers" not breastfeeding mothers.[10] Expressing breast milk and feeding it to a baby in a bottle has become more widespread, even for mothers staying at home. The motorized breast pump industry is booming, with the nation beginning to look like, in Lepore's words, "a giant human dairy farm." Pumping at work has become de rigueur:

> Duck into the ladies' room at a conference, of, say, professors and chances are you'll find a flock of women with matching "briefcases," waiting none too patiently and, trust me, more than a little sheepishly, for a turn with the electric outlet. Pumps come with plastic sleeves, like the sleeves in a man's wallet, into which the mother is supposed to slip a photograph of her baby, because, Pavlov-like, looking at the picture aids "let-down," the release of milk normally triggered by the presence of the baby, its touch, its cry.[11]

In this scenario, breast milk becomes a commodity to be pumped, bottled, and fed to the baby to improve its immune system or to ensure that it later achieves higher marks at school than (one assumes) a formula-fed baby. Breastfeeding has become detached from its association with warmth, intimacy, comfort, nurture, emotional well-being, or flesh against flesh. One wonders whether, at some stage in the future, we will look back at the vision of all this feverish pumping with the same abhorrence we do the use of wet nurses in the past.

In some respects, breast milk has always had a market value.[12] Just as privileged white mothers used to rely on wet nurses, so those professional women working at Goldman Sachs probably depend on other women, from different classes and cultures (like Mimi or Carmen, discussed in chapter 4) to feed the precious and hard-won "expressed milk" to their infants. While these racialized and class-based patterns of exploitation may be much the same as in the past, the mechanized processes of production are relatively new. The design of motorized breast pumps may appear to be personal, but their purpose is profoundly industrial: increasing productivity in the workplace. Breast-feeding and nurturing a child is one of many experiences mothers have after giving birth that *feels* entirely gendered. And I am sure that for women, expressing milk in a work break at dedicated "corporate pumping stations," this experience also makes them acutely aware of gender. The *New Yorker* article also makes clear that babies and toddlers are not allowed in these purpose-built lactation rooms, nor indeed in the workplaces that boast lactation policies as a sign of their dedication to gender equity. What does this tell us about the real agenda here? The industrialized lactating breast is thus unlinked from the baby its function is to feed. Breast-feeding is framed as a practical problem to be managed or overcome in the interests of maintaining productive workplaces.

Lepore asks what she describes as "a privately agonising and publicly unpalatable" question. Is it the milk or is it the mother that matters more to a baby?[13] What makes this question so "unpalatable" is the prevalence of gender-neutral perspectives in the public arena. According to a postmaternal, neoliberal cultural logic, care—including the care of babies—is seen to be a transferable (and a purchasable) commodity. A degendered answer to Lepore's question might be that the baby needs a combination of the milk and an attentive carer. Once again, to be blind to the embodied postbirth experience of the lactating mother is to be blind to gender. It also risks downplaying the possible emotional needs of women and newborn babies at this significant time. While such views are increasingly commonplace in the public sphere, they are also completely inadequate. Such gender-neutral feminist interventions fail to challenge the neoliberal policies that have been identified as imposing such cruel penalties on the most vulnerable in our society: children, the frail elderly, sole mothers, women both in the workforce and at home, and poor migrant women working in domestic labor and child care (as outlined in previous chapters). In my view, the only way to address this failure would be to reinvigorate the strands of feminism that are attuned to gender difference, however it may be conceived. A feminism that promotes gender neutrality under the guise of equality has proved vulnerable to the false promises of neoliberalism and has played a dispiriting role in limiting the formation of genuine social and policy alternatives.

Perhaps the limitations of a degendered feminism can be checked by the emergence of a theoretically informed "regendering" in new movements around feminism and environmental sustainability. In some respects these movements can be seen to be "actively remembering" the nurturing impulses of earlier maternalist campaigns. In other ways they intersect with some of the new expressions of maternalism in current peace activism and in the online mothers' movements. However, there are key differences in this regendering that may point to another way forward. One notable distinction is the explicit use of frameworks that draw directly on the feminist ethic of care tradition. This tradition, as I have indicated in earlier chapters, is usually traced to the work of Carol Gilligan's *In a Different Voice*, which identified "two ways of speaking about moral problems, two modes of speaking about other and self."[14] Certain ethical systems and ways of conceptualizing problems were seen to be more common to women, according to Gilligan. These included an interconnected sense of self and a morality more concerned with care, relationships, narrative, and contexts than one dedicated to rights, rules, autonomy, and abstract notions of justice. Subsequent responses to Gilligan's ideas have given shape to the feminist ethic of care tradition. The work of Nel Noddings, Sara Ruddick, Eva Feder Kittay, and Joan Tronto is usually given credit here, although it is important to note there are considerable variations between these theorists.[15] For the purposes of this conclusion, more recent theorizing about extending the radical potential of the care ethic to the "nonhuman" realm is of significance. Notably this has been evident in some contemporary approaches to animal ethics that link feminist understandings of the oppression of women to ways of thinking about the domination of animals.[16] Similarly, ecofeminist perspectives enlarge this view to include the natural environment. This view is premised on a rejection of hierarchical dualisms such as human/nature and man/woman and, following Gilligan, promotes a different way of thinking about other and self. According to Greta Gaard, in *Eco-feminism: Women, Animals, Nature*, the ideological processes that make the subordination of women, animals, and nature seem natural are the same processes. Thus "others" are both feminized and "animalized."[17] By contrast, the feminist care ethic reasserts the "fundamental interconnectedness of all life,"[18] and this has become the basis for an ecological, ethical, and critical theory.

There is a varied and engaging literature on the philosophy and limitations of ecofeminism. However, a sideways glance at a concrete and contemporary cultural development linking feminist care approaches to environmental ethics may prove illuminating here. Peggy Orenstein in the *New York Times* has recently identified the new phenomenon of the "femivore."[19] In "The Femivore's Dilemma," Orenstein provides examples of highly educated feminist women moving away from the workforce to home and community. The home is intentionally reconfigured as a "self-sustaining center of labor and livelihood for both sexes," with women playing a key role in raising children, chickens, growing clean food, and attempting to reduce consumption and the family's carbon footprint. A feminist inflection is given to the more established "locavore" movement of eating locally produced food and developing local food networks that include home gardens and community-based enterprises. The aim of developing more self-reliant and green food economies seems to have been taken up by feminists employing an ethic of care approach. Care for the environment, for plants, and for animals is seen to be integral to care for children and family and a resistance to market-driven, commercial processes and notions of identity. "Rather than embodying the limits of one movement, femivores expand those of another: feeding their families clean, flavorful food; reducing their carbon footprints; producing sustainably instead of consuming rampantly. What could be more vital, more gratifying, more morally defensible?"[20] Orenstein's article has been widely discussed online and recirculated in the print media both inside and outside the U.S. It draws on some of the research that informed Shannon Hayes's recent book *Radical Homemakers: Reclaiming Domesticity from a Consumer Culture*.[21] Naturally, reference to the term *homemakers* raises all kinds of uncomfortable ideological associations that hark back to the gender politics of the 1950s. This is reflected in some of the online responses to Orenstein's article, which ask whether the phenomenon of the femivore is a frontier throwback that will further add to the unequal domestic burden shouldered by women.[22] One response notes that the term *femivore* should really mean "someone who eats women."[23] Hayes's book, however, does not use this term at all to describe the creative intersection between feminism and environmentalism. She describes this development and the women she interviews as "rebuilding a life-serving, socially just and ecologically sustainable economy while honoring the values of feminism."[24] Elsewhere, in a similar vein, she refers to reclaiming domesticity as a "life nurturing" alternative to our existing consumer culture."[25]

While *Radical Homemakers* is more popular than scholarly in focus, it nonetheless represents a resistance to postmaternal thinking, an attempt to regender and reconfigure feminism in new and interesting ways. The central role of nurturing is explicitly reclaimed in relation to family and the environment, as the femivore example shows. Hayes also urges women and men to rebuild "home" as the moral, foundational unit of radical social change. There are interesting parallels between this approach and more theoretically informed feminist analyses. Joan Williams's *Unbending Gender: Why Family and Work Conflict and What to Do About It* is one example that comes to mind. Williams discusses the need for a "reconstructive feminism" where "raising children is not a private frolic of one's own."[26] In a chapter entitled "Do Women Share an Ethic of Care?" Williams notes the way domesticity has functioned, from its inception, as an "internal critique" of capitalism. "In a political culture, with few viable languages of critique, domesticity offers a Marxism you can bring home to mother, one of the few available languages with widespread vernacular resonance available for critiquing the excesses of liberal individualism."[27] This critique is expressed in various currents of the mothers' movement and also in certain branches of ecofeminism. Indeed, Hayes remodels the notion of domesticity so that its previous association with drudgery and domination is transformed into a shared resistance to consumer capitalism. It would seem that Williams is also right about the role of "vernacular gender-talk."[28] Feminism, according to Williams, is in effect a form of "gender-talk," and new ways of talking need to be invented so that descriptions of men and women "do not trigger gender wars among women with a different relationship to domesticity."[29] This seems to be borne out by new expressions of feminist peace activism, discussed previously. It is notable that, at a time when a gender-neutral feminism is dominant in the public sphere, using exaggerating symbols of gender seems to be uniting rather than dividing women. CODEPINK is one such example, and the femivore movement another. Perhaps this means that the gender-neutral language of feminist policy discourse has failed to take hold or resonate at the everyday level.

Where does a new maternalism fit in these frameworks? Why end this book by contrasting the corporate use of breast pumps (a degendered feminism) with femivores and their ethic of care for children and the environment (a regendered feminism)? I return once again to the work of Sara Ruddick, the touchstone throughout this investigation for all care-focused feminist theorizing and central to the ideas that have evolved in the preceding chapters. Ruddick ended her recent reflections on the twentieth anniversary of her book *Maternal Thinking* with what she described as a beginning; a complex contemporary interweaving of maternal thinking, peace, and care for the environment.[30] Many of the complicated threads that have emerged in the course of my book's exploration of memory, feminism, and postmaternal thinking come together in this interweaving, particularly in debates about the relationship between maternalist elements in ecofeminist peace politics. Some of these threads include widespread nostalgia for premarket relationships and identities or discomfort with the paid consumption of emotional services. Many display a deep cultural unease with abstract, genderless notions of possessive individualism disconnected from community and the natural world. Ecofeminism promises an alternative resolution to these tensions by resignifying nurture and care and extending it to the nonhuman world. However, just as with any movements in the past that have used mothering as a paradigm of social and political care, the problem of essentialism shadows any move forward. Niamh Moore highlights the dimensions of this problem:

> Ecofeminists are derided for allegedly suggesting that women's role caring for children may leave women more inclined to care for the planet too. Ecofeminism seems to have reignited anxieties which perhaps have lain dormant given the commonly assumed demise of peace activism. Such a reading of feminist peace activism, and ecofeminism, collapses a more complicated politics of non-violent activism into manifestations of maternalism, and then further collapses maternalism into essentialism. Essentialism is then one of the key concepts on which many eco/feminisms are seen to flounder, particularly activist eco/feminisms.[31]

As previously indicated, essentialism is the charge that all women (and in this case, mothers) share a single, universal relationship to care and nurture and, in this case, to nature. While much more diversity is borne out by the everyday experience of individual women, the fact remains, as Eva Feder Kittay puts it, that most women are occupied by caring for their dependents at some point, and for many women "this occupies the better part of their lives."[32] Yet, as Moore so clearly points out, "challenging biological determinism and other essentialisms has been a crucial policy strategy for feminists."[33] Consequently, any activism done in the name of the maternal will be unsettling, particularly for those who perceive feminism as primarily a struggle against essentialism. Moreover, given the prevalence of postmaternal thinking in the wider culture, maternalism remains an uncomfortable and ambiguous political configuration. However, as I have tried to argue, this in itself does not make thinking maternally wrong or inappropriate either to social policy or to moves toward a new politics. Returning to Carol Adams's unequivocal assertion, "I value nurturing and caring because it is good, not because it constitutes women's 'difference.'"[34]

Crucially, pejorative accusations of essentialism have "closed questions of women and nature and feminism and pacifism" and "been posed as an impasse for feminism," according to Niamh Moore.[35] Her examination of ecofeminist peace politics suggests that it is time to move beyond this impasse. In my view, this means not reproducing the class-based, racialized, nationalist, and conventional maternalism of the past. New online mothers' movements go some way to doing this. Yet, they can also be limited by conceptions of motherhood as an identity or subject position unrelated to nurturing and care for children, as outlined in chapter 4. It would seem that, rather, the task is to actively remember maternal thinking as the paradigm for an alternative model of social and political life. This model, following Ruddick, extends the notion of "preservative love" as far as to include "the needs and pleasures of any animal or plant."[36] As a form of practice-based reasoning, it resists essentialism by respecting what Ruddick describes as "unpredictable and as yet, unimagined difference."[37] It also contests the "women as Nation Builders" version of second-wave feminism (discussed in chapter 3), particularly as it relates to state-sanctioned war and violence.

Some of the more recent and imaginative scholarship around mothering and feminism is making advances in this direction. For instance, Andrea O'Reilly, through her many publications in the area, always presents mothering as "an explicitly and profoundly political-social practice, transformative and transgressive."[38] Similarly, social philosopher Anne Manne suggests the possibility of a new supple, flexible kind of feminism, independent, with an "unblinking eye," that can respond to "new circumstances, new problems."[39] She sees hope in the emergence of new genres of maternal feminism. These new developments, according to Manne, build on "earlier feminist arguments," but also go beyond them. Acknowledging the wider implications of Ruddick's notion of "maternal thinking," Manne stresses the importance of "attempting to translate into practical politics the values of 'caritas': the care for others on a par with—if not above—concern for 'oneself,' including the care for other people's children, not just one's own, as well as other vulnerable citizens."[40]

Why then, in so many other contexts, does embracing the possibility of such a newly configured feminist maternalism still seem to raise the specter of essentialism and visions of the narrow ideological frameworks associated with the prefeminist maternalism of the past? Aside from these examples, ecofeminism appears to be one of the few theoretical and political interventions not queasy about the maternal. It resists the directive to "leave motherhood behind" in what is conventionally considered to be the path to an activist future. The intersection between feminism, environmentalism, and peace politics can therefore be portrayed not as a trace of the old but as a site through which an alternative feminist politics can be imagined.[41]

On the other hand, it would be easy to become caught up in the rhetoric and romanticism of feminist sustainability movements like the femivores or radical homemakers and forget that these developments emerge from sites of great affluence, globally speaking. It is important to remember that this particular variety of ecofeminism is dependent on having the material space (land) to bring a different model of feminist community into being. It would be wrong to lose sight of the fact that most people live in large cities such as New York, Tokyo, Cairo, Shanghai, or São Paulo, and it remains to be seen whether ecofeminism can provide any kind of relevant alternative to these populations. Similarly, it is too early to say whether ecofeminist activism and gendered responses to climate change can provide a different model of maternalism that avoids the risks of essentialism. However, such initiatives do raise significant questions about the specificities of any new and distinct "feminist maternalism." How would such an approach be framed in the context of the environmental crisis; neoliberal welfare "reform," which has taken a heavy toll on the most vulnerable in society including women and children; the policy dominance of a degendered feminist politics; and, finally, conceptions of "self" so closely identified with the instrumentality of the marketplace? Speculation can only be partial and provisional, pointing toward alternative possibilities rather than any sort of blueprint. Unlike the maternalism of the past, perhaps current expressions of a new maternalism would be more collective and not focused on individual agency. Following the examples of groups such as Mothers Acting Up or CODEPINK, they would have an international dimension and reflect the character of contemporary global social movement networks (see chapter 4). In my view, maternalism as a formation outside the boundaries of the nation-state would be a very different creature to that of the maternalist campaigns in the early part of the twentieth century and may bring into being a more inclusively global maternal politics.

For all the reasons outlined in this conclusion, a new feminist maternalism cannot be blind to gender difference, regardless of how socially constituted that difference may be. Gender-neutral perspectives produce overly cognitive and abstract understandings of the human self and risk denying the materially embodied nature of motherhood. Actively remembering the bodily and emotional aspects of nurture, including the physical demands of birth, lactation, and the postnatal experience, will pave the way for more just social policies for women and families. There is no doubt that different policy approaches need to be urgently developed to enable both women and men to arrange their lives around care, not only care for children and other dependents but also allowing themselves to be cared for at times of vulnerability and need. This would involve challenging political structures of forgetting that have led to "dependency"as a deviant condition, or as a failure of will, rather than as an inescapable part of the life cycle. If the practice and analysis of cultural memory can itself be a form of political activism, then remembering nurture, care, and the inevitability of dependency can signal ways to encourage more open-ended dialogues about feminism and maternalism.

Notes

PREFACE

1. See Plant's *Mom* for an excellent discussion of reformulations of the dominant maternal ideal over the twentieth century.
2. Gavigan and Chunn, "Introduction," 7.
3. For an excellent discussion of theses debates in the wake of the financial crisis, see Peck, Nik, and Brenner, "Postneoliberalism and Its Malcontents."
4. Gavigan and Chunn, "Introduction," 2.
5. Ruddick, *Maternal Thinking*.
6. Aside from Ruddick's own *Maternal Thinking*, other striking examples include Eva Feder Kittay's chapter about her daughter, "'Not *My* Way Sesha, *Your* Way, Slowly': A Personal Narrative," in her influential *Love's Labor*, 147–62. Anne Manne also integrates the personal with great delicacy in *Motherhood*.
7. Mezey and Pillard, "Against the New Maternalism."

INTRODUCTION

1. The radio discussion with Halpern, author of *The Etiquette of Illness* is at "Learning the Skill of What to Say in a Moment of Illness."

2. Kittay, *Love's Labor*, 29.

3. Hirsch and Smith, "Feminism and Cultural Memory," 6.

4. Orloff, "From Maternalism." It should be noted that at the time of completing this book Orloff was also finishing a manuscript entitled "Farewell to Maternalism? State Policies, Social Politics, and Mothers' Employment in the U.S. and Europe."

5. Orloff, "From Maternalism," 230.

6. Ibid.

7. See chapter 4 for a more detailed discussion of these debates and the specific theorists involved.

8. I have greatly benefited here from the clear overview of central debates about maternalism by reading Eirinn Larsen's thesis "Gender and the Welfare State: Maternalism as New Historical Concept," Department of History, University of Bergen, Norway, 1996, http://www.ub.uib.no/elpub/1996/h/506002/eirinn/eirinn.html.

9. Ladd-Taylor, *Mother-Work*, 3.

10. Koven and Michel, "Introduction."

11. Plant, *Mom*.

12. Ibid., 3.

13. Ibid., 7.

14. Ibid., 8.

15. See Sennett, *The Culture of the New Capitalism*.

16. Aside from *The Culture of the New Capitalism*, also see Sennett, *The Corrosion of Character* and *The Craftsman*.

17. Sennett, *The Culture of the New Capitalism*, 5.

18. Mosher, "Intimate Intrusions," 165.

19. Manne, "Motherhood and the Spirit of the New Capitalism," 66; also see Manne, "Love and Money" and "The Question of Care."

20. Interview with Sennett, "Big Ideas."

21. For a good discussion of this idea, see Meyers, "Introduction."

22. Young, "Autonomy, Welfare Reform, and Meaningful Work," 42.

23. For a discussion of this theorization of dependence, see DiQuinzio, *The Impossibility of Motherhood*, 10.

24. Clark, *Epic Change*, 60.

25. Connerton, *How Societies Remember*.

26. See Barbara Czarniawska-Joerges, "The Narrative Turn in the Social Sciences," in Czarniawska-Joerges, *Narratives in Social Science Research*, 1–15.

27. Hirsch and Smith, "Feminism and Cultural Memory."

28. Ibid., 5.

29. Connerton, "Seven Types of Forgetting," 60–71.

30. Ibid., 62–64.

31. Ibid., 63.

32. Ibid.

33. Ruddick, *Maternal Thinking*.

34. Ibid., 40–41.

35. Ibid., 123.

36. Sara Ruddick, in O'Reilly and Ruddick, "A Conversation About Maternal Thinking," 17.

37. Kittay, *Love's Labor*.

38. Aside from Ruddick, see Gilligan, *In a Different Voice*; Noddings, *Caring*; Tronto: *Moral Boundaries*.

39. Hirsch and Smith, "Feminism and Cultural Memory," 13.

40. O'Reilly, *Mother Matters*, 20.

41. Hochschild, "'Rent a Mom.'"

1. UNMOTHERING

1. Ruddick, *Maternal Thinking*, 56.

2. Orloff, "From Maternalism," 232.

3. O'Connor, Orloff, and Shaver, *States, Markets, Families*.

4. Orloff, "From Maternalism," 230–68.

5. Ibid., 254 (see figure 6.1).

6. Mezey and Pillard, "Against the New Maternalism," 47.

7. Williams, *The Constraint of Race*.

8. Ibid., 277.

9. Orloff, "From Maternalism," 232.

10. See the discussion of Sennett in my introductory chapter.

11. Olrloff, "From Maternalism," 241.

12. Fraser and Gordon, "A Genealogy of Dependency."

13. Cusk, *A Life's Work*, cited in Ruth Quiney, "Confessions of the New Capitalist Mother," 28.

14. Interview with Sennett, "Big Ideas."

15. West, "The Right to Care," 88–89.

16. Williams, *Unbending Gender*, 41.

17. Eisenstein, "A Dangerous Liaison?" 488.

18. Fraser, "Feminism, Capitalism."

19. Eisenstein, "A Dangerous Liaison?" 488.

20. Ibid., 491.

21. Ibid., 495.

22. Ibid., 498.

23. Fraser, "Feminism, Capitalism," 107.

24. Eisenstein, "A Dangerous Liaison?" 509.

25. Ibid., 511.

26. Eisenstein, *Feminism Seduced*.

27. Eisenstein, "A Dangerous Liaison?" 509.

28. Ibid., 510.

29. Ibid., citing Gimenez, "Connecting Marx and Feminism."

30. Ibid., 488.

31. Fraser, "Feminism, Capitalism," 97.

32. See, for example, Fraser, "After the Family Wage."

33. Fraser, "Feminism, Capitalism," 114.

34. See ibid., note 12.

35. See Leela Gandhi's *Postcolonial Theory*, 42–43, for a discussion of the new humanities as those interdisciplinary areas which foreground the exclusions inherent in canonical knowledge systems and, secondly, which aim to recover marginalized knowledges. Postcolonialism, gender studies, cultural studies, and ethnography would be included in her definition.

36. Ruddick, *Maternal Thinking*, 130. See also Donovan and Adams, *The Feminist Care Tradition in Animal Ethics*.

37. Ruddick, *Maternal Thinking*, 134.

38. See revised preface to the 1995 edition of *Maternal Thinking*, xi.

39. For an excellent analysis of Ruddick's idea of the maternal and her notion of preservative love, see DiQuinzio, *The Impossibility of Motherhood*, 119–24.

40. See, for an early response, Rumsey, "Constructing Maternal Thinking."

41. Aanerud, "The Legacy of White Supremacy."

42. See Bailey, "Mothering, Diversity," 188–99.

43. DiQuinzio, *The Impossibility of Motherhood*, 120.

44. See Gilligan, *In a Different Voice*.

45. Ruddick, "Rethinking 'Maternal' Politics," 370.

46. See my introduction.

47. O'Reilly, *Maternal Thinking*. See also the special issue of *Women's Studies Quarterly* on mothering, particularly section 6, "Classics Revisited: Sara Ruddick's *Maternal Thinking: Toward a Politics of Peace*," *Women's Studies Quarterly* 37, nos. 3 and 4, (2009): 295–308.

48. DiQuinzio, "Mothering Without Norms?" 104.

49. Andre, "The Virtue of Honoring Oneself," 79.

50. O'Reilly and Ruddick, "A Conversation About Maternal Thinking."

51. Once again, see Orloff's "From Maternalism."

52. Connerton, "Seven Types of Forgetting," 63.

53. Interview with Sennett, "Big Ideas."

2. FEMINIST REMINISCENCE

1. See Segal, *Making Trouble*, 87–89.

2. Dux and Simic, *The Great Feminist Denial,* 7.

3. Fraser, "Feminism, Capitalism," 114.

4. Walker, *Baby Love*, 168.

5. See http://www.npr.org/templates/story/ (accessed July 8, 2009).

6. Sturken, *Tangled Memories,* 1–7.

7. See Halbwachs, *On Collective Memory.*

8. For a good discussion of Halbwachs, see Green, *Cultural History,* 104–7.

9. Hirsch and Smith, "Feminism and Cultural Memory," 7.

10. de Marneffe, *Maternal Desire*, 23.

11. Hirsch, *The Mother/Daughter Plot.*

12. Ruddick, *Maternal Thinking*, xxvi.

13. Manne, *Motherhood*, 61.

14. Ibid., 62.

15. Roiphe, *A Mother's Eye*, 19.

16. Hirsch, "Feminism at the Maternal Divide," 354.

17. Ibid., 355.

18. Ibid., 365.

19. Reddy, Roth, and Sheldon, *Mother Journeys*, 1.

20. Cited by Roiphe, *Mother's Eye,* 18.

21. Segal, *Making Trouble,* 1–11.

22. Cox, interviewed by Ann-Marie Jordens.

23. Ann Snitow, "A Gender Diary" quoted in Henry, *Not My Mother's Sister*, 8.

24. Phyllis Chesler, *Letters to a Young Feminist*, quoted ibid., 9.

25. Ibid., 9.

26. See, for example, Walker, "Becoming the Third Wave," 39–41, and *To Be Real*; Wolf, *Fire with Fire*; Denfeld, *The New Victorians*.

27. See Henry, *Not my Mother's Sister*, 14.

28. While I use the generational terms, I agree with Astrid Henry that the notion of a "cohesive generational unit is always a fiction"; see Henry, *Not My Mother's Sister*, 6.

29. Henry, *Not My Mother's Sister*, 46.

30. Hallstein, "My Mother's Gift of Feminism."

31. Ibid.

32. Clift, "I Am A Feminist," 222.

33. Walker, *Baby Love*, 6.

34. Ibid., 46.

35. The ideas in Haussegger's "The Sins of Our Feminist Mothers." It is important to note that this article is still being cited in discussions about the legacy of feminism.

36. Hausseger, *Wonder Woman*, 25. See also Campo, "Having It All.."

37. Wolf, *Misconceptions*; Crittenden, *What Our Mothers Didn't Tell Us*.

38. Showden, "What's Political About the New Feminisms," 180.

39. Dean, "Who's Afraid of the Third Wave."

40. Douglas and Michaels, *The Mommy Myth*, 32.

41. Dux and Simic, *The Great Feminist Denial*, 98.

42. See ibid., 118. The authors also include a discussion of a culture of antimotherhood permeating the second wave and cite noted feminist and historian Ann Curthoys who comments that at the time a less supportive atmosphere for mothers can scarcely be imagined; ibid., 111–12.

43. Campo, *From Superwoman to Domestic Goddess*, 4–6.

44. Ibid., 6.

45. Campo describes Leslie Cannold as "bravely" taking stay-at-home mothers to task (ibid., 111). Cannold's promotion of a degendered feminism will be discussed in the conclusion.

46. Campo, *From Superwoman to Domestic Goddess*, 103.

47. Ibid., 97.

48. See Manne, *Motherhood*, 158–83, and "Love and Money," 77.

49. For details, see Manne, "Love and Money," 76–79.

50. See Segal, *Making Trouble*, 83–90.

51. de Marneffe, *Maternal Desire*, 131.

52. Elshtain, "The Communitarian Individual," 99–109.
53. Ibid., 104.
54. Lanoix, "The Citizen in Question," 114.
55. Interview with Sennett, "Big Ideas."
56. Ibid.
57. See Hochschild, *The Time Bind.*
58. Ehrenreich and Hochschild, *Global Woman*, 5.
59. Etzioni, *The Spirit of Community*, 56.
60. Brenner and Haaken, "Utopian Thought," 338.
61. Elshtain, "The Communitarian Individual," 105.
62. Cusk, *A Life's Work*, 130.
63. Gurtler, "The Ethical Dimension of Work, "127.
64. Kittay, "A Feminist Public Ethic of Care," 527.
65. Connerton, "Seven Types of Forgetting," 63.
66. Ibid., 63.
67. Roiphe, *Mother's Eye*, 4.
68. See Roiphe, "My Newborn Is Like a Narcotic." The ensuing controversy can be found at http://www.salon.com/mwt/broadsheet/feature/2009/08/27/roiphe_motherhood/index.html.
69. Garner, "Maternal Boundaries," 69–70.
70. See DiQuinzio, *The Impossibility of Motherhood*, xix, 243.
71. Such as Wolf, *Misconceptions*; Cusk, *A Life's Work*; or Walker, *Baby Love.*
72. Wolf, *Misconceptions*, 7.
73. Johnson, *A Better Woman*, i.
74. Ibid., 19.
75. Quiney's "Confessions," 35.
76. Cusk, *A Life's Work*, 7, quoted ibid., 21.
77. Ibid., 31–32.
78. Wolf, *Misconceptions*, 64–65, quoted by ibid., 29.
79. Belkin, *Life's Work*. Such titles seem to be an industry in their own right in the U.S. and include Buchanan's *Mother Shock* and Halliday's *The Big Rumpus.*
80. Cusk, quoted by Quiney, "Confessions," 32.
81. Johnson, *A Better Woman*, 19.
82. See chapter 1 and also Orloff, "From Maternalism," 232.
83. Hochschild, *The Commercialization of Intimate Life*, 7.
84. See, of course, Ruddick's *Maternal Thinking.*
85. Manne, *Motherhood,* 57.

1. See Cusk, *A Life's Work*, 136; Johnson, *A Better Woman*, 19; Naomi Wolf, *Misconceptions*, 64–65.
2. See Bornat and Diamond, "Women's History and Oral History," 21.
3. As examined by Youngblood Jackson in "Rhizovocality," 696.
4. Williams, "I'm a Keeper of Information," 44.
5. Hochschild, *The Commercialization of Intimate Life*, 7.
6. See Sawer, *Sisters in Suits;* and Watson, *Playing the State.*
7. Segal, *Making Trouble*, 32.
8. The National Library of Australia Oral History Collection contains a wide range of interviews with well-known Australian women who were active in the women's liberation movement. This includes writers, historians, academics, public commentators, activists, and those who achieved considerable success in the political and executive arenas. While some of the interviews to be discussed here were conducted with this aim firmly in view, others were part of oral projects on Australian feminist historians, political activists, academics, or women members of parliament and the senior bureaucracy.
9. Thomson "Four Paradigm Transformations in Oral History," 50.
10. As discussed by Green, "Individual Remembering," 35.
11. See for example, Stanley and Wise, *Breaking Out.*
12. Thomson citing Daniel James's *Dona Maria's Story: Life History, Memory and Political Identity* in "Four Paradigm Transformations in Oral History," 64.
13. For a discussion of the idea of composure and how gender intersects with culture and memory see Summerfield, "Culture and Composure."
14. Thomson, *Anzac Memories,* 9, also cited by Green in "Individual Remembering," 40.
15. Summerfield attributes the concept to Graham Dawson in *Soldier Heroes*, see "Culture and Composure," 69.
16. Summerfield, "Dis/composing the Subject."
17. Bellamy, interviewed by Ward.
18. Ibid.
19. Ibid.
20. Suzanne Bellamy worked on this first women's liberation newspaper, *Mejane,* which was published from 1971–1974.

21. Bellamy.

22. For an exception to this view, see Henderson, *Marking Feminist Times*.

23. Curthoys, *Feminist Amnesia*, 4.

24. Ibid., 7.

25. Ibid., 5.

26. Matthews, *Good and Mad Women*.

27. To borrow a phrase from Henderson, "The Tidiest Revolution," 186.

28. Matthews, interviewed by Ward.

29. Henderson, "The Tidiest Revolution," 187.

30. Modjeska cited by Henderson, "The Tidiest Revolution," 183.

31. Ibid., 185.

32. Ibid., 180.

33. See, for example, Echols, *Daring to Be Bad*, and *Shaky Ground*. See also Jo Freeman in a posting to the H-Women network situating the three main waves of feminist activism in periods of organized agitation for social change such as abolitionism, progressivism, and "the Sixties," arguing that each has been shaped by the movements which gave them birth, see http://www.jofreeman.com/feminism/waves.htm.

34. Echols, *Shaky Ground*, 1.

35. Henderson, "The Tidiest Revolution,"187.

36. Ibid., 181.

37. Ibid., 178.

38. Gitlin, *The Sixties*, 433.

39. See Green, "Individual Remembering," 35–44.

40. Ibid., 36.

41. Ibid., 37.

42. Kansteiner, "Finding Meaning in Memory," 180.

43. Burgmann, interviewed by Turner.

44. Magarey, interviewed by Dowse.

45. Comment by Sara Dowse in the Magarey interview 2008.

46. Dowse and Magarey conversing in the Magarey interview (my emphasis).

47. Segal, *Making Trouble*, 1.

48. Ibid., 61.

49. Gorton, "Theorizing Emotion and Affect," 345.

50. Ruddick, *Maternal Thinking,* see in particular the new preface to the 1995 edition, xx.

51. Marilyn Lake's entry in Caine et al., *Australian Feminism,* 133.

52. See Lake, *Getting Equal*.

53. Ruddick, *Maternal Thinking*, xxi.

54. See, for the definition of maternalism I have used in previous chapters, Koven and Michel, *Mothers of a New World*, 4–5.

55. Johnson, interviewed by Turner.

56. As a contrast, see the language of Murray, *More Than Refuge*, 48.

57. Johnson interview.

58. Ward, interviewed by Dowse.

59. Ryan, interviewed by Dowse.

60. Benhabib, "From Identity Politics to Social Feminism."

61. See, for example, the seminal essay by Ann Snitow that pinpoints a pronatalist theme in different stages of the women's liberation movement, "Feminism and Motherhood." See also Evans, *Tidal Wave*, 55–56.

62. Green, "Individual Memory," 35–45.

63. Segal, *Making Trouble*, 89–90.

64. Dowse, interview by Ward.

65. Margaret Talbot, "Supermom Fictions," *New York Times Magazine*, October 27, 2002, 11–12, cited in Parkins, "Shall I Be Mother," 66.

66. See Quiney, "Confessions of the New Capitalist Mother," 31.

67. Dowse interview (1997, 1998).

68. See Curthoys, *Feminist Amnesia*.

4. MATERNALISM RECONFIGURED?

1. An impressive range of these publications, festivals, and events (including the Museum of Motherhood) can be found at the Web site for Mamapalooza at http://www.mamapalooza.com (accessed March 24, 2010).

2. Jessela, "Mom's Mad" (accessed March 2, 2010).

3. Koven and Michel, "Introduction," 4.

4. Wilkinson, "The Selfless and the Helpless," 573.

5. Ibid., 583.

6. Mink cited ibid., 583.

7. Skopcol, *Protecting Soldiers and Mothers*, 2.

8. Wilkinson, "The Selfless and the Helpless," 578.

9. Ruddick, *Maternal Thinking*, 25.

10. Ibid.

11. O'Reilly, "Feminist Mothering as Maternal Practice," 217.

12. See, for example, Salon.com at http://www.salon.com/mothers/mamaf-esto.html and Brain Child at http://www.brainchildmag.com.

13. For example, groups like Mumsnet played a role in the British elections; see http://www.mumsnet.com. For Australian examples, see Motherhugger: motherhood activism Australia at http://motherhugger.blogspot.com/2010/03/workshop-on-feminist-mothering-and.html.

14. See the article in the *Times* at http://www.timesonline.co.uk/tol/comment/columnists/rachel_sylvester/article6919267.ece (accessed April 6, 2010).

15. Lopez, "The Radical Act of 'Mommy Blogging," 730.

16. Ibid., 733.

17. Ibid.

18. Friedman and Calixte, *Mothering and Blogging*.

19. For an overview, see Tucker, "Small World."

20. See http://www.mothersactingup.org/about/sub-page-in-about-section (accessed March 31, 2010).

21. See, for example, http://www.mothersactingup.org/issues.

22. Wieviorka, "After New Social Movements."

23. See http://www.mothersactingup.org/about/principles.

24. See http://mothersandmore.org.

25. http://www.mothersandmore.org/AboutUs/member_statistics.shtml (accessed April 1, 2010).

26. Tucker, "Motherhood and Its Discontents."

27. Mamapalooza (mampalooza.com) would be one such example. A group that does not conform to this categorization would be Moms Rising (momsrising.org), where children (and family) are more at the forefront of the activism expressed through their Web site. This group targets congressional and state-level policies in areas such as family leave, environmental policy, or health reform and took what it ambitiously describes as over one million actions last year alone; see http://www.momsrising.org/aboutmomsrising.

28. Mezey and Pillard, "Against the New Maternalism," 3.

29. See http://www.mamapalooza.com/home.html (accessed April 2, 2010).

30. See http://www.museumofmotherhood.org (accessed April, 2, 2010).

31. Ruddick, *Maternal Thinking*, xi.

32. Sara Ruddick's comments in O'Reilly and Ruddick, "A Conversation About Maternal Thinking," 17.

33. Linker, "Explaining the World," 41.

34. Ruddick in O'Reilly and Ruddick, "A Conversation About Maternal Thinking," 30.

35. The Watch Out for Children site expired on March 20, 2010, and is pending renewal or deletion.

36. Tucker, "Motherhood and Its Discontents," and "An Interview with Enola Aird" (accessed March 9, 2010).

37. Aird interview at http://www.mothersmovement.org/features/Aird_interview.htm.

38. Ibid.

39. Stadtman Tucker, "Motherhood and Its Discontents,"4.

40. Ibid.

41. Hays, *The Cultural Contradictions of Motherhood*, 8.

42. Ibid.

43. Ruddick in O'Reilly and Ruddick, "A Conversation About Maternal Thinking," 33.

44. Ibid.

45. Douglas and Michaels, *The Mommy Myth*, 4.

46. Ibid.

47. See Plant's excellent analysis of account of Philip Wylie's *Generation of Vipers*, his misogynist idea of *momism*, and its influence at the time in *Mom*, 19–32.

48. This seems to be the case in the Mothers' Movement conferences. See, for example, the program for the conference "Representing Motherhood: Mothers in the Arts, Literature, Media, and Popular Culture," from the Motherhood Institute for Research and Community Involvement (replacing the Association for Research on Mothering), May 20–22, 2010. Also see the conference program for "Amplifying (M)other's Voices 2010" sponsored by mamapalooza, the Museum of Motherhood, and the Motherhood Foundation, http://www.motherhoodmuseum.org/MOMConference4.html.

49. O'Reilly in O'Reilly and Ruddick, "A Conversation About Maternal Thinking," 35.

50. Ruddick, ibid., 33.

51. See DiQuinzio, "Mothering Without Norms?" Also, in the same collection, Guzmán, "Mothers Working Together for Peace"; and Pershing, "Cindy Sheehan."

52. Ruddick, "Epilogue and a New Beginning."

53. See the reference in Allen, *Feminism and Motherhood in Western Europe*, 133.

54. Ruddick, *Maternal Thinking*, 154, 156.

55. "What We're Fighting For: A Letter from America," at http://www.american-values.org/html/wwff.htmlt (accessed April 17, 2010).

56. Ibid.

57. See, for example, Ruddick's comments: "Women have never absented themselves from war . . . [and have supported] the military engagements of their sons, lovers, friends and mates"; Ruddick, *Maternal Thinking*, 154.

58. See Scheper-Hughes, "Maternal Thinking and the Politics of War." See also DiQuinzio's reading of Scheper-Hughes in "Mothering Without Norms?"

59. See http://www.codepink4peace.org/ (accessed April 25, 2010).

60. Starhawk's comments at http://www.codepink4peace.org.

61. See http://www.alternet.org/action/146441/.

62. For a more detailed discussion of this kind of politics, see Stephens, *Anti-Disciplinary Protest*.

63. Goss and Heaney, "Organizing Women as *Women*."

64. Ibid., 28.

65. Ibid.

66. Ibid., 32.

67. See Sheehan, "Mama's Don't Let Your Babies" (accessed April 26, 2010).

68. Pershing, "Cindy Sheehan," 146.

69. Quoted ibid., 152–53.

70. Cockburn, "Gender Relations," 143.

71. Ibid.

72. Cockburn, "Getting to Peace" (accessed January 7, 2011).

73. Bailey, "Mothering, Diversity, and Peace," 163.

74. Strong, *The Maternal is Political*, 9.

75. Ibid., 10.

76. Walker, "The Maternal Is Sustainable," 219–25.

77. Sheehan, "Good Riddance."

78. See http://www.cindysheehanssoapbox.com (accessed May 10, 2010).

79. Sheehan, "Good Riddance," 261.

80. Ibid., 262.

81. Ibid., 263.

82. Masterson, "Alien," 25–30.

83. See, for example, Sassen, *Globalization and Its Discontents*; Bales, *The Slave Next Door*; Sassen, "The Other Workers."

84. Kozol, "Filming the Care Chain."

85. See Poo, "Domestic Workers Bill of Rights."

86. Anderson, "A Very Private Business," 258.
87. Quoted ibid., 254.
88. Ibid., 255.
89. Ehrenreich and Hochschild, *Global Woman*.
90. Arlie Russell Hochschild, "Love and Gold," in Ehrenreich and Hochschild, *Global Woman*, 17.
91. Quoted ibid., 24.
92. Ibid., 15.
93. Advertisement in the *Sunday Age Magazine*, February 1, 2009, 3.
94. See Stephens, "Motherhood and the Market," "Eyes Wide Shut in the Childcare Debate," "Beyond Binaries in Motherhood Research."
95. Manne, *Motherhood*.
96. See Wilson and Lande, "Feeling Capitalism," 275.
97. Anderson, "A Very Private Business," 254.
98. Hochschild, in Wilson and Lande, "Feeling Capitalism," 276.
99. Hochschild, "'Rent a Mom.'"
100. Ibid., 79.
101. Gillis, "Our Imagined Families," 2.
102. Ibid.
103. Garber, *Sex and Real Estate*, quoted in Gillis, "Our Imagined Families,"2.
104. Hochschild, "'Rent a Mom,'" 77.

CONCLUSION

1. See Orloff, "From Maternalism."
2. Lanoix, "The Citizen in Question," 114.
3. Benhabib, "From Identity Politics to Social Feminism," 30.
4. Cannold, "Parents Left in the Lurch.
5. Cannold, "Baby Leave Is Not A Women's Issue."
6. This is closer to the universal breadwinner model proposed by Nancy Fraser, one of the three ideal types to follow the demise of the male/breadwinner, female homemaker model. According to the idea of the universal breadwinner, gender equity ensures all adults can engage in paid employment and care is marketized and/or outsourced. See Fraser, "After the Family Wage."
7. Fraser, "Will Feminism Be Articulated to the Left or to the Right" (accessed July 22, 2010).

8. My attention was drawn to this article in a seminar given by Ann Orloff at the Australian Social Policy Conference in Sydney in 2009. I am grateful for the insights Orloff provided in this seminar. Her presentation is recorded at http://www.abc.net.au/tv/bigideas/stories/2009/10/21/2720407.htm. The article by Lepore is titled "Baby Food."

9. Ibid.

10. See the wide responses online to Lepore's article.

11. Lepore, "Baby Food."

12. It is interesting to note that the breast fluid secreted directly after birth, colostrum, is now marketed and sold for its health properties as a powder to add to smoothies and shakes. One assumes that this breast substance is "harvested" from other mammals. However, it is not impossible, in a futuristic scenario, to imagine that this too (like the global trade in human organs) may become a commodity that impoverished women are forced to sell in a new, transnational form of wet-nursing. Colostrum products are advertised on an enormous number of Web sites. For example, "Buy 1 and Get 1 Free" at http://www.puritanspride.com.au/colostrum.

13. Again see Lepore, "Baby Food."

14. Gilligan, *In a Different Voice*, 1.

15. See Noddings, *Caring*; Kittay, *Love's Labor*; Tronto: *Moral Boundaries*.

16. See Donovan and Adams, *The Feminist Care Tradition*.

17. Gaard, "Living Interconnections with Animals and Nature," 8. Gaard here is referring to Adams, "The Feminist Traffic in Animals."

18. Ibid., 2.

19. Orenstein, "The Femivore's Dilemma" (accessed July 14, 2010).

20. Ibid.

21. Hayes, *Radical Homemakers*.

22. See, for example, http://www.grist.org/article/the-femivore-new-breed-of-feminist-or-frontier-throwback.

23. See, for example, http://gourmetfood.suite101.com/article.cfm/femivores-hegans-and-omnivores-oh-my.

24. Hayes, *Radical Homemakers*, 19.

25. Ibid., 50.

26. Williams, *Unbending Gender*.

27. Ibid., 195.

28. Ibid., 181.

29. Ibid., 183.

30. Ruddick, "Epilogue and a New Beginning."

31. Moore, "Eco/Feminism," 283.

32. Kittay, *Love's Labor*, 182.

33. Moore, "Eco/Feminism," 283.

34. Adams, "Caring About Suffering," 201.

35. Moore, "Eco/Feminism," 283.

36. Ruddick, *Maternal Thinking*, 130.

37. Ibid., 134.

38. O'Reilly, *Rocking the Cradle*, 13.

39. Manne, *Motherhood*, 30.

40. Ibid., 68.

41. Moore, "Eco/Feminism," 282.

Bibliography

Aanerud, Rebecca. "The Legacy of White Supremacy and the Challenge of White Anti-Racist Mothering." *Hypatia* 22, no. 2 (2007): 21–38.

Adams, Carol J. "Caring About Suffering: A Feminist Exploration." In Josephine Donovan and Carol J. Adams, eds., *The Feminist Care Tradition in Animal Ethics*, 198–229. New York: Columbia University Press, 2007.

—— "The Feminist Traffic in Animals." In Josephine Donovan and Carol J. Adams,, eds., *The Feminist Care Tradition in Animal Ethics,* 195–219. New York: Columbia University Press, 2007.

Allen, Ann Taylor. *Feminism and Motherhood in Western Europe, 1890–1970: The Maternal Dilemma*. New York: Palgrave, 2005.

Anderson, Bridget. "A Very Private Business: Explaining the Demand for Migrant Domestic Workers." *European Journal of Women's Studies* 14, no. 3 (2007): 246–64.

Andre, Judith. "The Virtue of Honoring Oneself." In Andrea O'Reilly, ed., *Maternal Thinking: Philosophy, Politics, Practice*, 79–91. Toronto: Demeter, 2009.

Bailey, Alison. "Mothering, Diversity, and Peace: Comments on Sara Ruddick's Maternal Thinking." *Journal of Social Philosophy* 25, no. 1 (1995): 162–82.

—— "Mothering, Diversity, and Peace Politics." *Hypatia* 9, no. 2 (1994): 188–99.

Bales, Kevin. *The Slave Next Door: Human Trafficking and Slavery in America Today*, Berkeley: University of California Press, 2009.

Belkin, Lisa. *Life's Work; Confessions of an Unbalanced Mom.* New York: Simon and Schuster, 2003.

Benhabib, Seyla. "From Identity Politics to Social Feminism." In Arthur M. Melzer, Jerry Weinberger, M. Richard Zinman, eds., *Politics at the Turn of the Century,* 27–42. Lanham, MD: Rowman and Littlefield, 2001.

Boris, Eileen. *Home to Work: Motherhood and the Politics of Industrial Homework in the United States.* New York: Cambridge University Press, 1994.

Bornat, Joanna, and Hanna Diamond. "Women's History and Oral History: Developments and Debates." *Women's History Review* 16, no. 1 (2007): 19–39.

Brenner, Johanna, and Janice Haaken. "Utopian Thought: Revisioning Gender, Family and Community." *Community, Work, and Family* 3, no. 3 (2000): 333–47.

Buchanan, Andrea. *Mother Shock: Loving Every (Other) Minute of It.* Berkeley: Seal, 2003.

Caine, Barbara. Moira Gatens, Emma Grahame, Sophie Watson, and Elizabeth Webby, eds. *Australian Feminism: A Companion.* Melbourne: Oxford University Press, 1998.

Campo, Natasha. *From Superwomen to Domestic Goddesses: The Rise and Fall of Feminism.* Bern, Peter Lang, 2009.

—— "Having It All or 'Had Enough': Blaming Feminism in *The Age* and the *Sydney Morning Herald,* 1980–2004." *Journal of Australian Studies,* no. 84 (2005): 63–72.

Cannold, Leslie. "Baby Leave Is Not a Women's Issue," *Age,* March 10, 2010.

—— "Parents Left in the Lurch," *Sydney Morning Herald,* January 4, 2010.

Clark, Timothy R. *Epic Change: How to Lead Change in the Global Age.* San Francisco: Wiley, 2008.

Clift, Rachel. "I Am a Feminist." In Susan E. Chase and Mary F. Rogers, eds., *Mothers and Children: Feminist Analyses and Personal Narratives,* 221–23. New Jersey: Rutgers University Press, 2001.

Cockburn, Cynthia. "Gender Relations as Causal in Militarization and War," *International Feminist Journal of Politics* 12, no.2 (2010): 139–57.

—— "Getting to Peace: What Kind of Movement?" at http://www.opendemocracy.net/5050/cynthia-cockburn/getting-to-peace-what-kind-of-movement.

Connerton, Paul. *How Societies Remember.* Cambridge: Cambridge University Press, 1989.

—— "Seven Types of Forgetting." *Memory Studies* 1, no. 1 (2008): 59–71.

Crittenden, Danielle. *What Our Mothers Didn't Tell Us: Why Happiness Eludes the Modern Woman.* New York: Touchstone, 2000.

Curthoys, Jean. *Feminist Amnesia: The Wake of Women's Liberation*. London: Routledge, 1997.

Cusk, Rachel. *A Life's Work: On Becoming a Mother*. London: Picador, 2003.

Czarniawska-Joerges, Barbara. *Narratives in Social Science Research*. London: Sage, 2004.

Dean, Jonathan. "Who's Afraid of the Third Wave." *International Feminist Journal of Politics* 11, no. 3 (2009): 334–52.

De Marneffe, Daphne. *Maternal Desire: On Children, Love and the Inner Life*. New York: Little, Brown, 2004.

Denfeld, Rene. *The New Victorians: A Young Woman's Challenge to the Old Feminist Order*. St Leonards: Allen and Unwin, 1995.

DiQuinzio, Patrice. "Mothering Without Norms? Empirical Realities and Normative Conceptions of Mothering." In Andrea O'Reilly, ed., *Maternal Thinking: Philosophy, Politics, Practice*, 104–20. Toronto: Demeter, 2009.

—— *The Impossibility of Motherhood: Feminism, Individualism, and the Problem of Mothering*. New York: Routledge, 1990.

Donovan, Josephine, and Carol J. Adams, eds. *The Feminist Care Tradition in Animal Ethics*. New York: Columbia University Press, 2007.

Douglas, Susan, and Meredith Michaels. *The Mommy Myth: The Idealization of Motherhood and How It Has Undermined All Women*. New York: Free Press, 2004.

Dux, Monica, and Zora Simic. *The Great Feminist Denial*. Carlton: Melbourne University Press, 2008.

Echols, Alice. *Daring to Be Bad: Radical Feminism in America, 1967–1975*. Minneapolis: University of Minnesota Press, 1989.

—— *Shaky Ground: The Sixties and Its Aftershocks*. New York: Columbia University Press, 2002.

Ehrenreich, Barbara, and Arlie Russell Hochschild, eds. *Global Woman: Nannies, Maids and Sex Workers in the New Economy*. London: Granta, 2003.

Eisenstein, Hester. "A Dangerous Liaison? Feminism and Corporate Globalization." *Science and Society* 69, no. 3 (2005): 487–518.

—— *Feminism Seduced: How Global Elites Use Women's Labor and Ideas to Exploit the World*. Boulder: Paradigm, 2009.

Elshtain, Jean Bethke. "The Communitarian Individual." In Amitai Etzioni, ed., *New Communitarian Thinking: Persons, Virtues, Institutions and Communities*, 99–109. Charlottesville: University Press of Virginia, 1995.

Etzioni, Amitai. *The Spirit of Community: The Reinvention of American Society*. New York: Simon and Schuster, 1993.

Evans, Sara M. *Tidal Wave: How Women Changed America at Century's End*. New York: Free Press, 2004.

Fraser, Nancy. "After the Family Wage: A Postindustrial Thought Experiment." In Nancy Fraser, ed., *Justice Interruptus: Critical Reflections on the "Postsocialist" Conditions*, 41–66. London: Routledge, 1997.

—— "Feminism, Capitalism, and the Cunning of History." *New Left Review* 56 (2009): 97–117.

—— "Will Feminism Be Articulated to the Left or to the Right: Nancy Fraser Interviewed by *European Alternatives*." http://mrzine.monthlyreview.org/2010/fraser170410.html.

Fraser, Nancy, and Linda Gordon. "A Genealogy of Dependency: Tracing a Keyword in the US Welfare State." In Eva Feder Kittay and Ellen K. Feder, eds., *The Subject of Care: Feminist Perspectives on Dependency*, 14–39, Lanham, MD: Rowman and Littlefield, 2002.

Friedman, May, and Shana L. Calixte, eds. *Mothering and Blogging: The Radical Act of the MommyBlog*. Toronto: Demeter, 2009.

Gaard, Greta. "Living Interconnections with Animals and Nature." In Greta Gaard, ed., *Ecofeminism: Women, Animals, Nature*, 1–13. Philadelphia: Temple University Press, 1993.

Gandhi, Leela. *Postcolonial Theory: A Critical Introduction*. St. Leonards: Allen and Unwin, 1998.

Garber, Marjorie. *Sex and Real Estate: Why We Love Houses*. New York: Pantheon, 2002.

Garner, Shirley Nelson. "Maternal Boundaries; or Who Gets 'the Lap.'" In Maureen T. Reddy, Martha Roth, and Amy Sheldon, eds., *Mother Journeys: Feminists Write About Mothering*, 65–70. Minneapolis: Spinsters Ink, 1994.

Gavigan, Shelley A. M., and Dorothy E. Chunn. "Introduction." In Shelley A. M. Gavigan and Dorothy E. Chunn, eds., *The Legal Tender of Gender: Law, Welfare, and the Regulation of Women's Poverty*, 1–15. Oxford: Hart, 2010.

Gilligan, Carol. *In a Different Voice: Psychological Theory and Women's Development*. Cambridge Massachusetts: Harvard University Press, 1982.

Gillis, John R. "Our Imagined Families: The Myths and Rituals We Live By." *The Emory Centre for Myth and Ritual in American Life: Working Paper* no. 7, 2002.

Gimenez, Martha. "Connecting Marx and Feminism in the Era of Globalization: A Preliminary Investigation." *Socialism and Democracy* 18, no. 1 (2004): 85–105.

Gitlin, Todd. *The Sixties: Years of Hope, Days of Rage*. New York: Bantam, 1987.

Gordon, Linda. *Pitied but Not Entitled: Single Mothers and the History of Welfare*. New York: Free Press, 1997.

Gorton, Kristyn. "Theorizing Emotion and Affect: Feminist Engagements." *Feminist Theory*, vol. 8, no. 3 (2007): 333–48.

Goss, Kristin A., and Michael T. Heaney. "Organizing Women as *Women*: Hybridity and Grassroots Collective Action in the Twenty-first Century." *Perspectives on Politics* 8, no. 1 (2010): 27–52.

Green, Anna. *Cultural History*. Hampshire: Palgrave Macmillan, 2008.

—— "Individual Remembering and 'Collective Memory': Theoretical Presuppositions and Contemporary Debates." *Oral History* 32, no. 2 (2004): 35–44.

Gurtler, Sabine. "The Ethical Dimension of Work: A Feminist Perspective." *Hypatia* 20, no. 2 (2005): 119–34.

Guzmán, Marguerite. "Mothers Working Together for Peace: Sara Ruddick and the Madres of the Plaza De Mayo." In Andrea O'Reilly, ed., *Maternal Thinking: Philosophy, Politics, Practice*, 133–44. Toronto: Demeter, 2009.

Halbwachs, Maurice. *On Collective Memory*. Trans. Lewis A. Coser. Chicago: Chicago University Press, 1992.

Halliday, Ayun. *The Big Rumpus: A Mother's Tales from the Trenches*. Berkeley: Seal, 2003.

Hallstein, Lynn O'Brien. "My Mother's Gift of Feminism with Sympathy but No Empathy." http://www.mothersmovement.org/essays/LOHallstein_0405.htm.

Halpern, Susan P. "Learning the Skill of What to Say in a Moment of Illness." http://www.abc.net.au/rn/newdimensions/stories/2008/2247167.htm.

—— *The Etiquette of Illness: What to Say When You Can't Find the Words*. New York: Bloomsbury, 2004.

Haussegger, Virginia. "The Sins of Our Feminist Mothers." *Age*, July 23, 2002.

—— *Wonder Woman: The Myth of "Having It All."* Crows Nest: Allen and Unwin, 2005.

Hayes, Shannon. *Radical Homemakers: Reclaiming Domesticity from a Consumer Culture*. Richmondville, NY: Left to Write Press, 2010.

Hays, Sharon. *The Cultural Contradictions of Motherhood*. New Haven: Yale University Press, 1998.

Henderson, Margaret. *Marking Feminist Times: Remembering the Longest Revolution in Australia*. Bern: Peter Lang European University Studies, 2006.

—— "The Tidiest Revolution: Regulative Feminist Autobiography and the De-Facement of the Women's Movement." *Australian Literary Studies* 20, no. 3 (2002): 178–91.

Henry, Astrid. *Not My Mother's Sister: Generational Conflict and Third Wave Feminism*. Bloomington: Indiana University Press, 2004.

Hirsch, Marianne. "Feminism at the Maternal Divide: A Diary." In Alexis Jetter, Annalise Orlek, and Diana Taylor, eds., *The Politics of Motherhood: Activist Voices from Left to Right*, 352–68. Dartmouth: University Press of New England, 1997.

—— *The Mother/Daughter Plot: Narrative, Psychoanalysis, and Feminism*. Bloomington: Indiana University Press, 1989.

Hirsch, Marianne, and Valerie Smith. "Feminism and Cultural Memory: An Introduction." *Signs: Journal of Women in Culture and Society* 28, no. 1 (2002): 1–19.

Hochschild, Arlie Russell. "'Rent a Mom' and Other Services: Markets, Meanings, and Emotions," *International Journal of Work, Organisation, and Emotion* 1, no. 1 (2005): 74–86.

—— *The Commercialization of Intimate Life: Notes From Home and Work*. Berkeley: University of California Press, 2003.

—— *The Time Bind: When Work Becomes Home and Home Becomes Work*. New York: Metropolitan, 1997.

Jessela, Kara. "Mom's Mad. And She's Organized." *New York Times*, February 27, 2007.

Johnson, Susan. *A Better Woman: A Memoir*. Milsons Point: Random House, 1999.

Jones, Gail. *Dreams of Speaking*. Milsons Point: Vintage, 2006.

Kansteiner, Wulf. "Finding Meaning in Memory: A Methodological Critique of Collective Memory Studies." *History and Theory* 41, no. 2 (2002): 179–97.

Kittay, Eva Feder. *Love's Labor: Essays on Women, Equality, and Dependency*. New York: Routledge, 1999.

—— "A Feminist Public Ethic of Care Meets the New Communitarian Family Policy." *Ethics* 111, no. 3 (2001): 523–74.

Koven, Seth, and Sonya Michel. "Introduction: 'Mother Worlds.'" In Seth Koven and Sonya Michel, eds., *Mothers of a New World: Maternalist Politics and the Origins of Welfare States*, 1–43. London: Routledge, 1993.

Kozol, Wendy. "Filming the Care Chain: A Review Essay." *Scholar and Feminist On-line* 8, no. 1 (Fall 2009). http://www.barnard.edu/sfonline/work/kozol_01.htm.

Ladd-Taylor, Molly. *Mother-Work: Women, Child Welfare, and the State, 1890–1939*. Urbana: University of Illinois Press, 1995.

Lake, Marilyn *Getting Equal: The History of Australian Feminism*. Sydney: Allen and Unwin, 1999.

Lanoix, Monique. "The Citizen in Question." *Hypatia* 22, no. 4 (2007): 116–29.

Lepore, Jill. "Baby Food: If Breast is Best, Why Are Women Bottling Their Milk?" *New Yorker*. January 19, 2009.

Linker, Maureen. "Explaining the World: Philosophical Reflections on Feminism and Mothering." In Andrea O' Reilly, ed., *Maternal Thinking: Philosophy, Politics, Practice*, 41–51. Toronto: Demeter, 2009.

Lopez, Lori. Kido. "The Radical Act of 'Mommy Blogging': Redefining Motherhood Through the Blogosphere." *New Media Society* 11, no. 5 (2009): 729–47.

Manne, Anne. "Love and Money: The Family and the Free Market." *Quarterly Essay*, no. 29 (2008): 1–90.

—— *Motherhood: How Should We Care for Our Children?* St. Leonards: Allen and Unwin, 2005.

—— "Motherhood and the Spirit of the New Capitalism." *Arena Journal*, no. 24 (2005): 37–67.

—— "The Question of Care." In David McKnight and Robert Manne, eds, *Goodbye to All That?: On the Failure of Neoliberalism and the Urgency of Change*, 147–81. Melbourne: Black, 2010.

Masterson, Sarah. "Alien." In Shari Macdonald Strong, ed., *The Maternal Is Political: Women Writers at the Intersection of Motherhood and Social Change*, 25–30. Berkeley: Seal, 2008.

Matthews, Jill Julius. *Good and Mad Women: The Historical Construction of Femininity in Twentieth-Century Australia.* Sydney: Allen and Unwin, 1984.

Meyers, Diana Tietjens. "Introduction." In Diana Tietjens Meyers, ed., *Feminists Rethink the Self*, 1–12. Boulder: Westview, 1997.

Mezey, Naomi, and Cornelia T. Pillard. "Against the New Maternalism." *Georgetown Law Faculty Publications and Other Works.* Paper no. 627. http://scholarship.law.georgetown.edu/facpub/627.

Mink, Gwendolyn. *The Wages of Motherhood: Inequality in the Welfare State, 1917–1943.* Ithaca: Cornell University Press, 1995.

Moore, Niamh. "Debating Eco/Feminist Natures." *International Feminist Journal of Politics* 10, no. 3 (2008): 314–21.

—— "Eco-Feminism, Non-Violence and the Future of Feminism." *International Feminist Journal of Politics* 10, no. 3 (2008): 282–98.

Mosher, Janet. "Intimate Intrusions: Welfare Regulation and Women's Personal Lives." In Shelley A. M. Gavigan and Dorothy E. Chunn, eds., *The Legal Tender of Gender: Law, Welfare and the Regulation of Women's Poverty*, 165–89. Oxford: Hart, 2010.

Murray, Suellen. *More Than Refuge: Changing Responses to Domestic Violence.* Perth: University of Western Australia Press, 2002.

Noddings, Nell. *Caring: A Feminine Approach to Ethics and Moral Education.* Berkeley: University of California Press, 1984.

O'Connor, Julia S., Ann Shola Orloff, and Sheila Shaver. *States, Markets, Families: Gender, Liberalism and Social Policy in Australia, Canada, Great Britain and the United States.* Cambridge: Cambridge University Press, 1999.

O'Reilly, Andrea. "Feminist Mothering as Maternal Practice: Maternal Authority and Social Acceptability of Children." In Andrea O'Reilly. ed., *Maternal Thinking: Philosophy, Politics, Practice,* 217–30. Toronto: Demeter, 2009.

O'Reilly, Andrea, ed. *Mother Matters: Motherhood as Discourse and Practice.* Toronto: Demeter, 2004.

—— *Rocking the Cradle: Thoughts on Feminism, Motherhood, and the Possibility of Empowered Mothering.* Toronto: Demeter, 2006.

O'Reilly, Andrea, and Sara Ruddick. "A Conversation About Maternal Thinking." In Andrea O'Reilly, ed., *Maternal Thinking: Philosophy, Politics, Practice,* 14–38. Toronto: Demeter, 2009.

Orenstein, Peggy. "The Femivore's Dilemma." *New York Times,* March 11, 2010.

Orloff, Ann. "From Maternalism to 'Employment for All': State Policies to Promote Women's Employment Across Affluent Democracies." In Jonah D. Levey, ed., *The State After Statism,* 230–68. Cambridge Massachusetts: Harvard University Press, 2006.

Parkins, Wendy. "Shall I Be Mother: Motherhood and Domesticity in Popular Culture." In Stacy Gillis and Joanne Hollows, eds., *Feminism, Domesticity and Popular Culture,* 65–79. New York: Routledge, 2008.

Peck, Jamie, Theodore Nik, and Neil Brenner. "Postneoliberalism and Its Malcontents." *Antipode: A Radical Journal of Geography* 41, supplement (2009): 94–116.

Pershing, Linda. "Cindy Sheehan: A Call to Maternal Activism in the Contemporary Peace Movement." In Andrea O' Reilly, ed., *Maternal Thinking: Philosophy, Politics, Practice,* 144–60. Toronto: Demeter, 2009.

Plant, Rebecca Jo. *Mom: The Transformation of Motherhood in Modern America.* Chicago: University of Chicago Press, 2010.

Poo, Ai-jen. "Domestic Workers Bill of Rights: A Feminist Approach for a New Economy." *The Scholar and Feminist On-line* 8, no. 1 (Fall 2009). http://www.barnard.edu/sfonline/work/print_poo.htm.

Prideaux, Simon. "From Organisational Theory to the New Communitarianism of Amitai Etzioni." *Canadian Journal of Sociology* 27, no. 1 (2002): 69–81.

Quiney, Ruth. "Confessions of the New Capitalist Mother: Twenty-First Century Writing on Motherhood as Trauma." *Women: A Cultural Review* 18, no. 1 (2007): 19–40.

Reddy, Maureen T. Martha Roth, and Amy Sheldon, eds. *Mother Journeys: Feminists Write About Mothering*. Minneapolis: Spinsters Ink, 1994.

Roiphe, Anne. *A Mother's Eye: Motherhood and Feminism*. London: Virago, 1997.

Roiphe, Katie. "My Newborn Is Like a Narcotic" (2009). http://www.doublex.com/section/kids-parenting/katie-roiphe-my-newborn-narcotic.

—— *The Morning After: Fear, Sex, and Feminism*. Boston: Little, Brown, 1994.

Ruddick, Sara. "Epilogue and a New Beginning." In Andrea O'Reilly, ed., *Maternal Thinking: Toward a Politics of Peace*, 252–71. Toronto: Demeter, 2009.

—— *Maternal Thinking: Toward a Politics of Peace*. Boston: Beacon, 1995 [1989].

—— "Rethinking 'Maternal' Politics." In Alexis Jetter, Annelise Orleck, and Diana Taylor, eds., *The Politics of Mothering: Activist Voices from Left to Right*, 369–82. Dartmouth: University Press of New England, 1997.

Rumsey, Jean P. "Constructing Maternal Thinking." *Hypatia* 5, no. 3 (1990): 125–31.

Sassen, Saskia. *Globalization and Its Discontents: Essays on the New Mobility of People and Money*. New York: New Press, 1999.

—— "The Other Workers in the Advanced Corporate Economy." *Scholar and Feminist On-line* 8, no. 1 (Fall 2009). http://www.barnard.edu/sfonline/work/print_sassen.htm.

Sawer, Marian. *Sisters in Suits*. North Sydney: Allen and Unwin, 1990.

Scheper-Hughes, Nancy. "Maternal Thinking and the Politics of War." In Lois Lorentzen and Jennifer Turpin, eds., *The Woman and War Reader*, 227–33. New York: New York University Press, 1998.

Segal, Lynne. *Making Trouble: Life and Politics*. London: Serpent's Tail, 2007.

Sennett, Richard. "Big Ideas." In *Under Ice Part 2.* http://www.abc.net.au/rn/big-ideas/stories/2007/1992673.htm.

—— *The Corrosion of Character: The Personal Consequences of Work in the New Capitalism*. New York: Norton, 1998.

—— *The Craftsman*. New Haven: Yale University Press, 2008.

—— *The Culture of the New Capitalism*. New Haven: Yale University Press, 2007.

Sheehan, Cindy. "Good Riddance, Attention Whore." In Shari Macdonald Strong, ed., *The Maternal Is Political: Women Writers at the Intersection of Motherhood and Social Change,* 260–64. Berkeley: Seal, 2008.

—— "Mama's Don't Let Your Babies Grow Up to Be Soldiers." http://www.truthout.org/article/cindy-sheehan-mamas-dont-let-your-babies-grow-up-be-soldiers.

Showden, Carissa R. "What's Political About the New Feminisms." *Frontiers* 30, no. 2 (2009): 166–98.

Skocpol, Theda. *Protecting Soldiers and Mothers: The Political Origins of Social Policy in the United States.* Cambridge: Harvard University Press, 1992.

Snitow, Ann. "Feminism and Motherhood: An American Reading." *Feminist Review* 40 (1992): 32–51.

Stanley, Liz, and Sue Wise. *Breaking Out: Feminist Consciousness and Feminist Research.* New York: Routledge, 1983.

Stephens, Julie. *Anti-Disciplinary Protest: Sixties Radicalism and Postmodernism.* Cambridge: Cambridge University Press, 1998.

—— "Beyond Binaries in Motherhood Research." *Family Matters,* no. 69 (Spring/Summer 2005): 96–101.

—— "Eyes Wide Shut in the Childcare Debate." *Arena Magazine* 50 (June/July 2001): 7–9.

—— "Motherhood and the Market." *Arena Magazine* 48 (August/September 2000): 35–37.

Strong, Shari Macdonald, ed. *The Maternal Is Political: Women Writers at the Intersection of Motherhood and Social Change.* Berkeley: Seal, 2008.

Sturken, Marita. *Tangled Memories: The Vietnam War, the Aids Epidemic, and the Politics of Remembering.* Berkeley: University of California Press, 1997.

Summerfield, Penny. "Culture and Composure: Creating Narratives of the Gendered Self in Oral History Interviews." *Cultural and Social History* 1, no. 1 (2004): 65–93.

—— "Dis/Composing the Subject: Intersubjectivities in Oral History." In Tess Coslett, Celia Lury, and Penny Summerfield, ed., *Feminism and Autobiography: Texts, Theories, Methods,* 91–107. New York: Routledge, 2000.

Sylvester, Rachel. "This Election Will Be Won at the School Gate Mum Power Matters. Politicians of All Parties Are Lining up to Test Their Family-Friendliness with the Voters on Mumsnet." *Times,* November 17, 2009.

Thomson, Alistair. *Anzac Memories: Living with the Legend.* Melbourne: Oxford University Press, 1994.

—— "Four Paradigm Transformations in Oral History." *Oral History Review* 34, no. 1 (2007): 49–70.

Tronto, Joan. *Moral Boundaries: A Political Argument for an Ethic of Care.* New York: Routledge, 1993.

Tucker. Judith Stadtman. "An Interview with Enola Aird." http://www.mothersmovement.org/features/Aird_interview.htm.

—— "Motherhood and Its Discontents: The Political and Ideological Grounding of the Twenty-first-Century Mothers Movement." http://www.mothersmovement.org/ . . . /jst_arm_presentation_10–04.pdf.

—— "Small World: Maternal Blogging, Virtual Friendship and the Computer-Mediated Self," In May Friedman and Shana L. Calixte, eds., *Mothering and Blogging: The Radical Act of the MommyBlog*, 1–20. Toronto: Demeter, 2009.

Walker, Rebecca. *Baby Love: Choosing Motherhood After a Lifetime of Ambivalence*. New York: Riverhead, 2007.

—— "Becoming the Third Wave." *Ms,* January/February (1992): 39–41

—— "The Maternal Is Sustainable." In Shari Macdonald Strong, ed., *The Maternal Is Political: Women Writers at the Intersection of Motherhood and Social Change,* 219–25. Berkeley: Seal, 2008.

—— *To Be Real: Telling the Truth and Changing the Face of Feminism.* New York: Anchor, 1995.

Watson, Sophie, ed. *Playing the State: Australian Feminist Interventions*. London: Verso, 1990.

West, Robin. "The Right To Care." In Eva Feder Kittay and Ellen K. Feder, eds., *The Subject of Care: Feminist Perspectives on Dependency,* 88–114. Lanham, MD: Rowman and Littlefield, 2002.

Wieviorka, Michel. "After New Social Movements." *Social Movement Studies* 4, no. 1 (2005): 1–19.

Wilkinson, Patrick. "The Selfless and the Helpless: Maternalist Origins of the U.S. Welfare State." *Feminist Studies* 25, no. 3 (1999): 571–97.

Williams, Joan. *Unbending Gender: Why Family and Work Conflict and What to Do About It.* New York: Oxford University Press, 2000.

Williams, Linda. Faye. *The Constraint of Race: Legacies of White Skin Privilege.* Philadelphia: Pennsylvania University Press, 2003.

Williams, Rhonda Y. "I'm a Keeper of Information: History Telling and Voice." *Oral History Review* 28, no. 1 (2001): 41–63.

Wilson, Nicholas Hoover, and Brian Jacob Lande. "Feeling Capitalism: A Conversation with Arlie Hochschild." *Journal of Consumer Culture* 5, no.3 (2005): 275–88.

Wolf, Naomi. *Fire with Fire: The New Female Power and How It Will Change the Twenty-first Century.* New York: Random House, 1993.

—— *Misconceptions: Truth, Lies, and the Unexpected on the Journey to Motherhood.* London: Chatto and Windus, 2001.

Young, Iris Marion. "Autonomy, Welfare Reform, and Meaningful Work." In Eva Feder Kittay and Ellen K. Feder, eds., *The Subject of Care: Feminist Perspectives on Dependency*, 40–60. Lanham, MD: Roman and Littlefield, 2002.

Youngblood Jackson, Alecia. "Rhizovocality." *International Journal of Qualitative Studies in Education* 16, no. 5 (2003): 693–710.

ORAL HISTORY SOURCES

Bellamy, Suzanne, interviewed by Biff Ward, National Library of Australia, recorded on March 10, 2000.

Burgmann, Meredith, interviewed by Ann Turner, National Library of Australia, recorded on January 18, March 9, and May 14, 2001.

Cox, Eva, interviewed by Ann Mari Jordens, National Library of Australia, recorded on April 19, 2002.

Dowse, Sara, interviewed by Ann Turner, National Library of Australia, recorded on December 22, 1997, and January 22, 1998.

Dowse, Sara, interview by Biff Ward, National Library of Australia, recorded on January 17, 1991.

Johnson, Phyllis, interviewed by Ann Turner, National Library of Australia, recorded on July 30 and September 17, 1995.

Magarey, Susan, interviewed by Sara Dowse National Library of Australia, recorded on November 17, 2008.

Matthews, Jill Julius, interviewed by Biff Ward, National Library of Australia, recorded on February 15, 2000.

Ryan, Julia, interviewed by Sara Dowse, National Library of Australia, recorded on September 26, 1990.

Ward, Biff, interviewed by Sara Dowse, National Library of Australia, recorded on September 24, 1998.

WEB SITES

AlterNet: On-line Independent News Magazine at http://www.alternet.org.

Brain Child: The Magazine for Thinking Mothers at http://www.brainchildmag.com.

Cindy Sheehan: Peace Activist at http://cindysheehanssoapbox.blogspot.com/.

Code Pink: Women for Peace at http://www.codepink4peace.org.

Institute for American Values at http://www.americanvalues.org/.

Jo Freeman: Feminist Scholar and Author at http://www.jofreeman.com/.

Mamapalooza: Awakening Mothers through Media, Commerce, Connection http://www.mamapalooza.com.

Moms Rising: Politics, Policy, Parenting at http://www.momsrising.org/about-momsrising.

MotherHugger: Motherhood Activism Australia at http://motherhugger.blogspot.com.

Mothers Acting Up: Advocating for the World's Children at http://www.mothers-actingup.org.

Mothers and Moore: Improving the Lives of Mothers at http://mothersandmore.org.

Mum's Net: By Parents For Parents at http://www.mumsnet.com.

Museum of Motherhood at http://www.museumofmotherhood.org.

National Public Radio: News, Analysis, World at http://www.npr.org/.

Open Democracy at http://www.opendemocracy.net.

Salon/Mothers Who Think at http://www.salon.com/mothers/mamafesto.html.

The Mothers Movement Online at http://www.mothersmovement.org.

The Scholar and Feminist On-line: Webjournal at http://www.barnard.edu/sfonline/.

Truthout: Progressive News Organization at http://www.truthout.org.

Index

Holding, 39–40

Home: autonomy from, 128; femivores for, 138–39; virtual, 130

How Societies Remember (Connerton), 8

H-Women network, 153n33

Identity: from child-bearing, 92–93; embedded self and, 60–64; motherhood and, 65–70; mothering as, 104; neoliberalism for, 31; politics of, 17; ultra-liberal self as, 60; workers compared to, 3, 12, 17, 22

The Impossibility of Motherhood: Feminism, Individualism, and the Problem of Mothering (DiQuinzio), 37–38

In a Different Voice (Gilligan), 137

Independence: dependence compared to, 23; support for, 24

Institute for American Values, 105, 112–13

Institute for American Values Mothers' Council, 106

Intensive mothering, 107–9

Interdisciplinary approach, xi, 14

Internet, *see* Maternal online community

James, Daniel, 76

Johnson, Phyllis, 89

Johnson, Susan, 67, 68–69

Jones, Gail, 71, 74

Justice: caring related to, 13, 63–64; economics associated with, 31–32

Just-war theory, 111; in Motherhood Project, 112–13

Kansteiner, Wulf, 82

Kittay, Eva Feder, 2, 13, 17; on essentialism, 11–12; on vulnerability, 63–64

Kollwitz, Käthe, 110–11

Koven, Seth, 4

Labor market: caregivers compared to, 19–20; neoliberalism associated with, x, 18–22

Lake, Marilyn, 88

Lanoix, Monique, 60

Lepore, Jill, 134–35

Liberation theory, 79

Linker, Maureen, 104–5

Literary Mama, 119

Locavore movement, 138

Lopez, Lori Kido, 99–100

Love: maternal, 65–69; maternal attentive, 112; mother, 5, 49, 65; *see also* Preservative love

Love's Labor: Essays on Women, Equality, and Dependency (Kittay), 11–12, 17

Maathai, Wangari, 111

Magarey, Susan, 84–86

Making Trouble: Life and Politics (Segal), 49–51, 86

"Mama Grizzlies," xiii

Mamapalooza, 104, 155n27

Manne, Anne, xv, 58, 70, 127, 145n6; on care, 12, 58; on fathers as caregivers, 58; on maternal feminist tradition, 46–47; on new capitalism, 6–7, 146n19, 150nn48–49; on new feminism developments, 142–43

Marneffe, Daphne de, 46, 59

Masterson, Sarah, 120–22

Maternal activism, 141–42; *see also* Feminist activism; Maternal nonviolent activism

Maternal attentive love, 112

Maternal Desire: On Children, Love, and the Inner Life (Marneffe), 46

Maternal feminist tradition, 46–47

Maternal identity; *see* Identity

Maternalism: antimaternalism, 5; buried, 87–94; contradictions within, 120–22; criticisms of, 96–97; cultural anxiety related to, 14, 43–44, 94; cultural manifestations of, 95–96; definitions of, ix, 3–4, 96; disputes regarding, 3–4; egalitarianism with, 115–16; farewell to, 19–20; feminism and, 105–7; feminist, 143–44; in feminist activism, 88–90; holding in, 39–40; intensive mothering and, 107–9; limitations of, 96–97; maternalist compared to, 5; in media, 95–96; memory studies for, xi–xii; momism in, 108–9; nationalism and, 112–13, 118; neomaternalism, 97–98; peace activism and, 16; private *versus* public, 4; romanticism of, 120–22; of Sheehan, 120; with a wink, 116; *see also* New maternalism; Postmaternalism

The Maternal Is Political: Women Writers at the Intersection of Motherhood and Social Change, 118–19

Maternalist feminist, 39–40

Maternal love, 65–69

Maternal nonviolence, 110–12

Maternal nonviolent activism: CODEPINK for, 113–15; history of, 115; pacifism compared to, 112; research on, 118; of Sheehan, 116–17, 119–20; *see also* Peace activism

Maternal online community: child-centered groups in, 100–102; CODEPINK as, 113–15; global groups of, 100–1; ideological roots of, 102; maternalist-dependency tension within, 102–3; mother-centered groups in, 101–2, 104, 155n27; new maternalism in, 103–4; participants in, 99–100; range of, 99–100; romanticism in, 103

Maternal thinking: afterlives and, 35–42; as alternative model, 142; disciplined reflection in, 36–37; environment and, 35–36; beyond mothers, 37–38; practicalism in, 36–37, 98–99; *see also* Maternal online community; Postmaternal thinking

Maternal Thinking: Philosophy, Politics, and Practice, 40, 110–11

Maternal Thinking: Toward A Politics of Peace (Ruddick), xii, 10–11, 37–41; ecofeminism in, 35–36; maternal nonviolence of, 110–12

practice, 36, 104–5; unmothering, 15, 132; war compared to, 111–12, 116–17
Motherlessness, 15
Mother love, 5, 49, 65
Mothers Acting Up, 144
Mothers Acting Up, 100–102
Mothers and Children: Feminist Analyses and Personal Narratives (Clift), 54–55
Mother's Day, 116, 119–20
A Mother's Eye (A. Roiphe), 48–49
Mothers & More, 101–2
Mothers' Movement conferences, 109, 156n48
Mothers Movement Online, 102
Mothers of a New World: Maternalist Politics and the Origins of Welfare States (Koven and Michel), 4
Mumsnet, 99

Nannies, 120–21, 123–24
Nationalism: maternalism and, 112–13, 118; matriotism compared to, 117; mothers for, 113, 157n57
National Library of Australia Oral History Collection, 51–52, 152n8; *see also* Oral histories
Nation Builders, 87, 94, 142
Neoliberalism, 19, 40; agelessness in, 60–61; for identity, 31; individualism related to, 66; labor market associated with, x, 18–22; policy related to, 17; postmaternalism and, 34–35, 71–72; in postmaternal thinking, x–xi, 34–35; second-wave feminism and, 31–32, 59, 93–94; Sennett

on, 60–61; social policy and, 18; unmothering and, 15; U.S. compared to Australia, 93
Neomaternalism, 97–98
New capitalism, 6, 7–8
New maternalism, xiii, 20, 118, 140; collectivity in, 144; ecofeminism in, 141; essentialism in, 141–42; gender neutrality in, 144; in maternal online community, 103–4; without men, 103
1966 Personal Responsibility and Work Opportunity Reconciliation Act, 20
Not My Mother's Sister: Generational Conflict and Third Wave Feminism (Henry), 46
Nurturing, 125; of children, 104–5; within feminist activism, 88–90

Obama, Barack, 30
O'Connor, Julia, 18–19, 22
Oral histories, 15–16; active remembering in, 83–84; aural value of, 84–86; of Bellamy, 77–79; of Burgmann, 82–83; career-activism alliance in, 90–91; challenges to, 78; close listening to, 73, 76, 84; composure in, 76–77; cultural scripts and, 82; of Dowse, 91–93; emotions in, 87; interactions during, 75–76, 78; of Johnson, P., 89; of Magarey, 84–86; of Matthews, 80; millennium related to, 75; mosaics within, 77–82; representation of, 74–75; of Ryan, J., 90; of Ward, 89–90

O'Reilly, Andrea, 14, 109–10, 142; Ruddick and, 40–41
Orenstein, Peggy, 138–39
Orloff, Ann, 2–3, 17–22, 146n4

Pacifism: feminist, 110; maternal nonviolent activism compared to, 112
Palin, Sarah, xiii, 34
Parenting: as gender neutrality, 11, 38; the term, 11, 38, 103–4
Peace: gender and, 111; *see also* Maternal nonviolence
Peace activism: maternalism and, 16; of Sheehan, 116–17, 119–20
Peace culture, 118
Pershing, Linda, 117
Personal narrative, 54–55; of author, xii–xiii; of Segal, 86–87; *see also* Oral histories
Pillard, Cornelia T., xiii, 20, 103–4
Plant, Rebecca Jo, 4–5
Policy: for lactation, 134–36; motherhood and, 16, 41; *Mumsnet*, 99; neoliberalism related to, 17; U.S. compared to Australia, 93; *see also* Social policy
Politics: of caring compared to work, 122–25; domesticity and, 139–40; domestic workers and, 122; of identity, 17
Postmaternalism: description of, 2–3; naturalization of, 22; neoliberalism and, 34–35, 71–72
Postmaternal thinking: antimaternalism compared to, 5; cultural anxiety and, 1, 41–42; definition of, ix–x, 22; dependence in, 7; as

ideology, 2; memory in, 6, 41–42; neoliberalism in, x–xi, 34–35; as pervasive cultural logic, x, 22; racialized social policy and, 20–21; thinking in, 36
Poverty: child poverty rates, 20; feminism and, 28–29
Power: cultural memory and, 2; exploitation and, 122–23
Practicalism, 36–37, 98–99
Preservative love, 11, 37, 39; of children, 41–42; extension of, 40; from nanny, 120–21; Ruddick on, 113
Profitability, 27–28

Quiney, Ruth, 67–68

Racialized social policy, 20–21
Radical Homemakers: Reclaiming Domesticity from a Consumer Culture (Hayes), 138
Responsive mothering, 109
Roiphe, Anne, 48–49, 65
Roiphe, Katie, 65
Rollin, Betty, 48
Ruddick, Sara, xii, 10–11, 17, 88, 140; active remembering for, 38–39; on children's vulnerability, 104–5; on ecofeminism, 35–36; framework of, 36–37; on intensive mothering, 108–9; on maternal nonviolence, 110–12; on maternal thinking, 98–99; on nationalism, 113, 157n57; O'Reilly and, 40–41; on preservative love, 113; relevance of, 35–37; on universal needs, 37